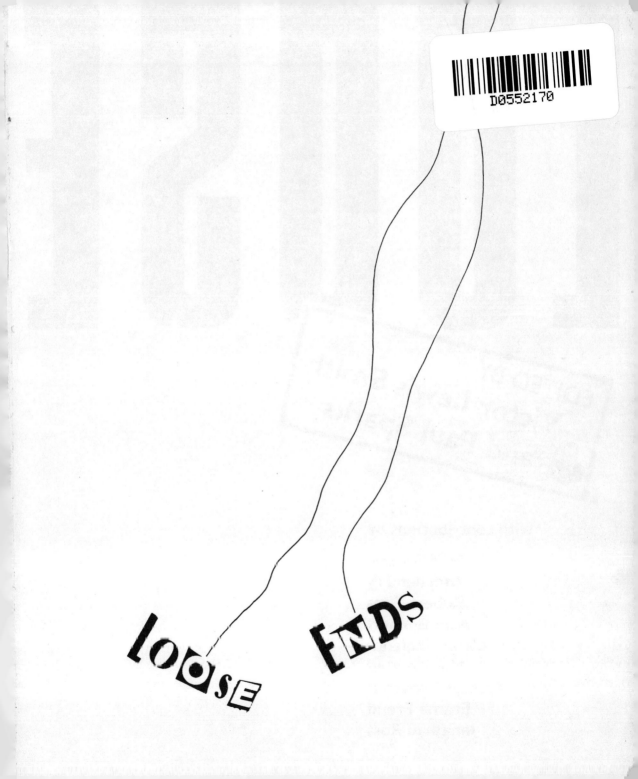

loOSe ENDS

LOOSE

EDITED BY
Victor Lewis Smith
and Paul Sparks

with contributions by

Ned Sherrin
Stephen Fry
Robert Elms
Alan Bennett
Carol Thatcher
Mat Coward
Frances Edmonds
Emma Freud
Jonathan Ross

ENDS

THE BOOK

EBURY PRESS
LONDON

☙ CONTRACT ☙

A contract made this 1st day of APRIL 1988

Between the members of the *Loose Ends* Radio Programme (hereinafter jointly called 'The Author') of the one part and Ebury Press, Colquhoun House, 27-37 Broadwick Street, London W1V 1FR (hereinafter called 'The Publishers') of the other part

WHEREBY IT IS MUTUALLY AGREED AS FOLLOWS:

1. The Author grants to the Publishers the sole and exclusive licence to print, publish and sell in book form in all languages throughout the world a new book edited by the Author and entitled provisionally

L O O S E   E N D S

(hereinafter called 'the work'), consisting of contributions from the regular members of the BBC Radio 4 programme.

2. The party of the first part shall be referred to as the party of the first part, but the Author solemnly swears not to fill up the book with recycled Marx Brothers' scripts.

3. Subject to legal advice, the Publishers agree to include eight (8) pages of 'tasteful and artistic poses' of Mr Sherrin in a state of deshabillé.

4. Unless otherwise mutually agreed the Author shall deliver the complete text to the Publishers not later than 31 December 1987. The Publishers agree to provide the Author with proofs of their work, and may demand from the Author proof that it is their own unaided work (e.g. a note from a parent or guardian) because we don't want any repetition of that unsavoury nonsense with Princess Michael, do we?

5. In the event that the Publishers consider the Author's manuscript to be a complete turkey, the Publishers reserve the right to put any or all of the following on the front cover of the book: a naked woman, a large £ sign, ' "This Book Changed My Life " —Noam Chomsky', another naked woman, an even larger $ sign, 'The Book they Tried to Ban', a picture of child songbird Toni Warne.

6. In the event that less than two hundred (200) copies of said book are sold, the Author and the Publishers shall indulge in mutual and acrimonious recriminations, the following phrases being deemed permissible: 'What the fxxx has your advertising department been doing for the past six months?', 'About as funny as being born dead with cancer' and 'I knew we should have gone to a proper publishers — Ebury? — we'd never have had this trouble if we'd gone straight to Faber.'

7. On publication, the Publishers shall send to the Author at the Author's home address ten (10) complimentary copies of the book, which will be piled up by the Author in the toilet where they will gather dust and get damp so that the covers curl up and eventually someone will be sick on them at a party.

8. When royalties are due to be paid the Publishers will produce, like a rabbit from a hat, a mysterious and previously unmentioned 'cover charge' (hereinafter referred to as 'the con') which will ensure that the Author receives what our legal boys refer to as 'bog all' (ls/4d).

9. There will be a special clause inserted into the contract, clause nine (9), which, in the contumacious impenetrability and intensity of its infrastructural nomenclature, with its tortuous determination of recondite allusion engendered by the sarmassophilic Kentucky colonels in our legal department, in its persistent and irremediable application of double, triple and even no, not never, not even quadruple (4) negatives and I agree to the con, will ensure that the Author, who only went to a comprehensive, will not understand what the hell he's signing but will sign anyway so as not to appear a complete dildo, the upshot of all this being that when royalties are due to be paid the Publishers will produce, like a rabbit from a hat, a mysterious and oh yes it was mentioned after all I didn't read all of clause nine (9) before, con which will ensure that the Author receives ls/4d.

10. The royalty cheque shall be deemed, at all times, to be in the post.

11. No royalties shall be payable from sales in Taiwan because the Publishers will only sell one (1) copy which will then be immediately pirated in photocopied editions and hawked about the island at half-price and the government will shrug their shoulders and say yes it is terrible but they don't know who's responsible, won't you, you thieving hypocritical slitty-eyed bastards?

12. The Author will spend much of his time amusing himself by trying to get words of dubious integrity, such as Tetbury portion, colpeurysis, osphresiolagnia and thelerethism into print, it being the job of the Publishers' proof readers to identify all such words, underline them in red ink, and to query their validity.

13. The books of account of the Publishers so far as they relate to any matter arising out of this agreement shall be open to inspection by the Author or the Author's duly authorised representative by appointment at any reasonable time, but you just try it on boyo, and we may just tip off the Inland Revenue about those tax-deductible business lunches with your so-called literary agent which always seem to take place in seedy hotels, and we all know which ten per cent (10%) of the Author she's getting, don't we dearie?

14. The Author hereby authorises and empowers the Author's agent to collect and receive all sums of money payable under the terms of this agreement from the Publishers.

15. There is one (1) born every minute.

signed by .... VICTOR → Bury

Simon Scott
EDITOR OF THE VERY FUNNY BOOKS
Ebury Press
London

BRITISH
BROADCA████ CORPOR████
TELE████ ██SE LON████
TELEGRAMS AND CABLES: BROADCASTS ████
PHONE 01-580 44██

Dear Simon,

I enclose our contract. Apart from the section about '████████ inspection' in Mr Hearst's office and the business about it 'feeling like a ████████ being stuffed into a dustbin', everything seems to be in order.

We look forward to receiving your cheque. As soon as we get it, our friend, Peter Langan, has promised to "take us on a f████ng rat-arse bender the likes you've never seen before", which we understand to mean a period of intense literary production for we realise that the deadline is approaching, and Mr. Langan says "all work and no play make Jack a ████████ dull boy give me your money".

Don't worry. We never miss a deadline, and after all, Nov. 2nd, 1988 gives us plenty of time me old fruit.

See you soon,

VICTOR
+ Rom

Victor and Paul

(PS: Pay us for last weeks visit, or we break your kneecaps)

PPS. Enclosed photos of us at our zhowbiz peak
as stars of Rediffusion TV's 'Christ I've burst
my bag' prezented by Muriel) Young

Published by Ebury Press
Division of The National Magazine Company Ltd
Colquhoun House, 27-37 Broadwick Street,
London W1V 1FR

First impression 1988

Designed by Harry Green
Illustrations by Derek Crowe and John Pead
Typeset by Typesetters Ltd, Stanstead Abbotts, Ware, Herts
Printed and bound in Great Britain by Butler & Tanner
Ltd, Frome and London

Photographic Credits

The authors and publisher would like to thank the
following for permission to reproduce material; while
every effort has been made to establish the copyright of
each picture, in some cases this has not been possible. The
authors and publisher would be grateful for any
information regarding the copyright of untraced items.
Barnaby's Picture Library: pages 14 (bottom right), 15
(bottom centre), 27, 53 (right), 57, 97 (top)
BBC Enterprises: Cover photographs, page 12
BBC Hulton Picture Library: pages 14 (top right), 53 (left)
Jan Croot: pages 98 (bottom), 99 (bottom left)
Daily Mail Film Award Annual: pages 16 (top), 24 (top),
40 (top), 60 (top), 80 (top), 100 (top), 188 (top)
Freemans Mail Order: page 118 (bottom)
John Frost Historical Newspaper Collection: pages 17
(left), 63, 97 (bottom left)
The Independent: pages 38-9
Popperfoto: pages 5, 11 (left), 40 (bottom left), 54, 58, 61, 70
(top and bottom right), 71 (centre and bottom right,
bottom left), 96 (left), 98 (top right), 100 (bottom left),
107, 110, 111, 120 (left)
Rex Features Ltd: 14 (top left), 15 (top left), 25 (top), 40
(bottom right)
Syndication International: 51 (top), 71 (centre left)
Topham Picture Library: 15 (top right), 33, 37, 70 (top and
bottom left), 96 (bottom left), 97 (bottom right), 120
(right)

AUTHORS' ACKNOWLEDGEMENTS

A zillion thanks are in order to Ronald Burnett for his
undying services to the British Empire and his vast
collection of printed ephemera; to Graham Pass for his
courage and foresight in commissioning the original Mr
Coaltart and risking life and limb we are eternally
grateful; to Simon Scott for his expertise, infectious
enthusiasm and encouragement; to Ian, Cathy, Simon,
Tina and the lot of them in the Loose Ends office; and to
David Harding, head of the BBC who, if not mentioned,
will give us no further work.

They're all good eggs and you can go into the jungle with
them.

Introduction

I shudder to think what is contained
between these sordid covers but
then I always shudder before listening to Victor Lewis Smith's and
Paul Sparks's *Loose Ends* pieces.
Sometimes unravelling of the
tape brings delight and hurts not
(but not always). The only con-
structive advice I can offer the
purchaser is to pick up this
book with a pair of fire-tongs
and hold it away from the
person at a safe distance.

Enjoy — as some people say.

NED SHERRIN

Victor — if this is too short print it twice

Introduction

I shudder to think what is contained
between these sordid covers but
then I always shudder before listening to Victor Lewis Smith's and
Paul Sparks's *Loose Ends* pieces.
Sometimes unravelling of the
tape brings delight and hurts not

Contents

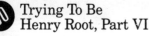
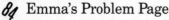

A week in the life of a Loose Ends producer

by the nice Mr Gardhouse

MONDAY

The crack of dawn. A three-mile jog, followed by a set of rigorous exercises — I use the Canadian Air Force System. Then a sip of black coffee (no sugar), a slice of wholemeal toast (no butter), then twenty-three press-ups, then...

The alarm clock says 11.30 a.m., and wakes me up from what's been an exhausting dream! So exhausting, in fact, that I decide to sleep on for another two hours. Frankly, I'm pooped!

I'm in the *Loose Ends* office *spot on* after lunch, all ready to start 'making radio baby' (as I say to the programme secretary, who wants an attachment to television pretty soon).

Post-mortem on Saturday's programme with my Editor who, it is rumoured, was a pretty nifty reserve goalkeeper for the Hungarian national football team in 1956. He was happy with the theme 'The Sinking of the Titanic', but thought some of the guests — especially Lena Zavaroni, Reg Varney, the man who does the voice-overs for the Cointreau ads, and a woman who once met Stephen Sondheim in a lift — 'lacked protein'. Try again.

TUESDAY

Over breakfast I read my advance copy of *Pig Farmer's Monthly* and muesli over a few philosophical bagatelles on the nature of Life, the Universe, and Radio 4 talk shows. Producing a talk show (never 'chat') is rather like being a puppet master. I'm in complete control. I pull the strings, I choose and book the five Pinocchios who sit around the table, I decide the subjects they will discuss, and for how long. Then, at precisely 10.02 every Saturday morning, in walks somebody from Bastards HQ holding a big pair of shears, cuts the strings, and says, 'Okay boys, take no notice of the fat bloke behind the glass with the beard and the flared trousers, go your own way, so long as it's very, very dull'. The philosophy gives me a headache so I take a Philosan.

goal

football

goal-keeper

Time for work. I don my sultry black leather jacket, studded with the legends 'DOES HE TAKE SUGAR?' and 'HATCH IS KING'. Leaving my luxurious Park Lane flat, I leap into my smart Sinclair C5 (with GT stripes on the side) and hurtle towards Broadcasting House at a steady 4 m.p.h. The beauty of the C5 is that I can drive straight into Reception, past the saluting commissionaires, and straight into the lift. There, chatting with the popular singing group Motorhead, is Margaret Howard, on her way to the Radio 1 'Acid Rock' studio, where she says she is the guest presenter. She too is looking for an attachment in television.

Once in the office I crack an hilarious joke about piles and, almost in the same breath, announce the theme for next Saturday's programme: 'You Get Yer Good 'N' Yer Bad In All Folks'. I immediately book Isla St Clair and Reg ('Mr Personality') Varney. By 5.30 I'm exhausted, so I rush off to the BBC Club bar for a pre-prandial sherry. Unfortunately, the drink is ruined, since I am propositioned by a Welsh actor with a most unsavoury suggestion. Hanging's too good, frankly.

WEDNESDAY

Decide to breakfast in the seventh floor canteen, but they tell me that lunch has already finished, so I tuck into one of their very splended health-giving banana and pilchard wholefood 'crumbles'. Yum yum! Seconds for me please!

The serving lady tells me she's looking for an attachment to the London Weekend Television canteen.

Back in the office, the telephone rings non stop, almost always publishers, who I insult in a thorough no-nonsense fashion. All is well until 4.30, then, *horror of horrors!* A call from Reg Varney's agent. Reg has just been booked by the Wogan Show. Naturally, nothing must compete with, or get in the way of, the good Mr Wogan, so I acquiesce and, turning to the talk show Bible (the *Reader's Digest*), search for a new theme.

5.30 and I 'strike oil' (as we say in radio). It's a biggy. The theme will be 'Ruptured...? I'm on top of the World!' By 6.30, all the guests are booked, so, dabbing some 'Homme Sauvage' behind my ears, I make for the BBC Club Drama Society where I've landed the role of eponymous hero in a play called *Waiting for Godot*. Since I'm not called on stage *at all* throughout the evening, I decide to have a glass of Wincarnis and practise moving in a mysterious way in the lobby of BH. A commissionaire attempts to escort me from the building, so I decide to call the police.

THURSDAY

I'm asked to leave my luxurious Pentonville cell at 8 a.m., after a night of 'good honest coppering',

The police

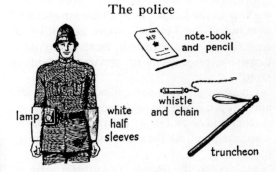

and hobble back to the office. My researcher, who is looking for an attachment in television, breaks some catastrophic news on the 'rupture' front. All my guests have been sucked, like so much plankton, into the Wogan Whale. So...bang goes Tammy Wynette, President Zia of Pakistan, Monty Modlyn, Nina and Frederick, Luciano Berio and the Singing Postman. 'That's showbiz', as we say in radio.

Later in the afternoon, my researcher remarks that my work output has increased by 2,000% this week. I explain that I have been requested by the

Editor of the *Loose Ends* book to contribute this piece. This is a bare-faced lie. I beseeched him on my bended knees to let me write something, in a death-or-glory bid to heighten my media profile, and so further my career in the BBC.

But still no programme.

FRIDAY

'Feeling good and walking tall', as we say in radio. By shaving off my beard and donning my old school uniform, I manage to appear as a contestant on *Blockbusters*, where the excellent Mr Bob Holness awards me a *Blockbusters* Dictionary and a *Blockbusters* Sweatshirt. Overcome with emotion, I drop them into the litter bin in the TV studio foyer.

Later, as I walk over the drunken heaps of *Start the Week* staff in the Kafkaesque corridors of BH, I am handed a note from someone in an ill-fitting uniform. It is a message from my researcher, who informs me that Ned Sherrin will be standing in for Wogan on Monday, and will need to spend all weekend in the Make-Up room as a team of cosmeticians attempt to undo the ravages of time. Cripes...no presenter! What pickles we get into in radio!

Quick as a flash I'm on the blower to the friendly and not-at-all jumped-up London Management Agency and book Freddy ('Parrot Face') Davies who agrees to front the show only if he's allowed to either:

a) expose the Hegelian synthetic view of history, or

b) plug his latest recording, 'Blippy Blippy Bloo Blah, I'm a silly parrot'. I opt for the latter and we talk money. He will accept luncheon vouchers. I've been tough, but I've been fair with him. Not for nothing do the top artistes call me Joe Blunt. Wheeling and dealing is my game.

I seek solace in a glass of Cherry B. And so to bed.

SATURDAY

In the office at 8.45 a.m. A note from my researcher. Freddie ('Parrot Face') Davies has dropped out on medical grounds. Being trained to deal with these last-minute difficulties, I stick my thumb into my mouth, utter the magic word 'Mummy' and adopt the foetal position. I dream of an attachment in television. Not too demanding, maybe Director of the Test Card with Music. Nothing else. Just that. I'd breeze in every morning with my black roll-neck sweater (gold

medallion nestling in my clip-on chest hair), change my name to Julian, and get the little girl into position (on her mark, as we say in television). Teddy to the left of her, blackboard to the right of her. I'd ask her to smile, cue the orchestra and shout 'Action...let 'em roll.') Seven hours later I shout 'Cut' and go home. Not terribly creative, but I'm told that the ratings are good.

9.00 a.m. Ned Sherrin nudges me awake and relief floods through me. The whole week has been a terrible dream, and we laugh together at the clichéd finish to this diary. I brief him on this morning's programme. The theme — 'The Sinking of the Titanic'. Guests, Lena Zavaroni, Reg ('Mr Personality') Varney, the man who does the voice-overs for the Cointreau ads, and a woman who once met Stephen Sondheim in a lift.

MEMO FROM THE DESK OF THE DIRECTOR GENERAL.

Dear Gardhise,

As you know, one of the conditions under which Herself is allowing us to continue broadcasting is that we cut costs rather dramatically. It has come to my attention that Loose Ends is one of our more expensive programmes, and frankly I can't see why; strikes me the whole thing could be wrapped up in five minutes flat a week without losing any of its essential wit, style, humour and originality - and that's including a four and a half minute theme tune. For a start let's get rid of the writers; I've never quite grasped what it is that writers do on a radio show, or anywhere else for that matter, so off they go. Here's the new schedule:

Ned can read the same monologue every week - so no change there. But can't we cut it down to just the one, quintessential joke? How about "Mr Kinnock is a smelly poo"? I always find that one goes down well. Then straight on to the taped reports. We'll have Robert Elms saying "I wear Levi 501's" and if you like we could have some taped guest saying "You've been in Barcelona too long, Bob, no-one wears them anymore". Then that Lewis Smith chap can ring up some crippled old woman who's just buried her husband that morning and pretend to be hubby, not dead at all - that shouldn't take more than about 4 seconds if we cut out all those fake dialling noises. Friend Coward's piece can be cut right back: just have him walk up to a famous person at a party and say "So you don't think I'd make a good Queen of England, then?" and have some famous person replying "Who are you?" and with that I think young Mat could more or less call it a career really, don't you?

As for Craig Charles - what exactly is it he does? And couldn't he just do it at home? The same goes for all the female chaps, frankly: repeat fees notwithstanding, all we actually need to do is tape them giggling and simpering in the background the once, and run it under Ned on every subsequent show. Or is that in fact what you do already?

Anyway, these are just a few helpful suggestions, and I hope you'll take them in the spirit in which they're intended. Not that it matters much how you take them, since I'm planning to replace you with your secretary anyway. Oh yes, I've heard all about how she puts the programme together single-handedly while you lot are down the pub all day. She told me herself.

Yours economically,
Tesco Checkout,
Director General (a.k.a. Mat Coward).

Ned Sherrin

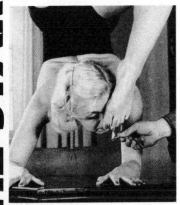

The youngest member of the team, said by legend to be the Beeb's original 'Auntie'. 'My job is to sort of hold it all together. I suppose you'd call me a kind of chairman or moderator' jokes Ned, one of Britain's foremost satirists, adding, with that wicked glint to the eye which has brought down more governments than Joe Gormley, 'We … er … we move ON!'

Jonathan Ross

Jonathan — or Jon Jon as he likes to be called by complete strangers in wine bars, should you ever have the pleasure of

bumping into him — was an obscure TV presenter when 'discovered' by *Loose Ends* producer Ian Gardhouse. Since then he has gone on to become one of the radio's most distinctive voices (only occasionally confused with Carol Thatcher). 'I'm very grateful for the chance to show what I can do,' says Jo-Jo, 'especially since my TV career doesn't seem to be going anywhere.'

Carol Thatcher

Despite the formidable obstacles of a tough, Northern, working-class upbringing, Carol has made it to the very top of her profession — doing the dirty jobs on *Loose Ends* that no-one else will touch. 'I'm not proud,' accepts Carol, 'just proud to be good at what I do.' Distinguishable on radio from Jonathan Ross because she rarely wears a tie.

Craig Charles

Little is known of this shy, retiring enigma. 'My low profile is deliberate,' says 'Craig'. 'I think that a lot of the kiddies

who tune in would be disappointed if they found out that I am in reality a white, 67-year-old, one-legged Old Etonian with a rare collection of Victor Sylvester 78s.'

Robert Elms

Known as 'The King of Style,' Bob is best known for being the prince of style.

Victoria Mather

'I love doing *les neds*,' chirps this cheerful Geordie lass, 'only the other day I went up to a complete stranger in t'Co-op and said "I'm on radio". "Oh really", he said, "which one are you?". "I'm the posh bird who

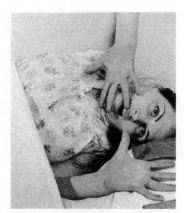

giggles in the background on *Loose Ends*," I replied. "Are you, be buggeree" he said, "well that narrows it down a bit". They're very direct in the North, that's why I find them so sweet.'

Mat Coward

In reality, a suave, sophisticated playboy with greying temples. Mat says 'I'm on the show to represent the ordinary man in the street — but I can't say anymore 'cos it's *sub judice*. The ordinary man in the street is suing the BBC for libel, slander and malicious misrepresentation.'

Victor Lewis Smith

Soft-spoken Vic puts his unique comedy style down to school bullying — 'I got a taste for it then,' he says

Emma Freud

Best known as the posh bird who giggles in the background on *Loose Ends*, Emma is also an accomplished hostess and one of London's most sought after escorts.

Frances Edmonds

Was a complete nonentity until she met Ned Sherrin in a Salvation Army soup kitchen queue. He introduced her to her future husband, Phil (the renowned leg spinner), and also gave her a hot bath, some decent clothes, some broth with a stale bread roll and a job on *Loose Ends*. She now has her pride back as a very sickeningly successful author who makes

more money than the editors of this little *pot-pourri*.

Stephen Fry

'I've never actually been on Loose Ends,' admits popular funny-man Steve, 'but they pay me £30,000 a year to use my name in the *Radio Times* billing.'

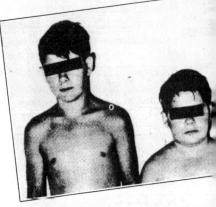

Nigel Farrell

'I got out while the going was good,' reminisces Nige, 'and I've never looked back.' Lucky bastard.

HAROLD COALTART
BBC COMMISSIONAIRE

Hello, won't beat about the bush. I am Mr Big at the BBC. You want to see Margaret Howard? Then see me first. I see them all in the foyer at Broadcasting House — Louise Botting, Ned Sherrin in his tie-dye vest, that Gardhouse in his Sinclair C5 driving into the lift, Robert Elms in his flared trousers — all the greats of Broadcasting, and Steve Race.

My name is Coaltart, Harold Coaltart, and round these parts people call me Harold Coaltart. Frankly, I live in the fast lane. Number 32, Fast Lane, Warley, actually. It was a council house ... we decided to buy ... I've knocked everything through. We've got a patio, a beautiful three-piece Draylon suite, and louvre windows. Course, I went for aluminium frames. I find them both economical and pleasing to the eye, and it does make our house stand apart from the, let's call them pond filth, who drink their money away down the beer shop, and consequently are still dealing with the council tallyman. P'raps I'm old-fashioned.

What an extraordinary week it's been for me. Cut a long story short, it all started Sunday lunchtime. I'd been commissioning that

Our superb Draylon suite purchased from a catalogue. 45 weeks @ 7/6 per week.

morning. The DG arrived and, as he passed me, I reminded him that the BBC is a democratic organisation and that all its employees have a right to be heard. Why, I quizzed him, don't they bring back *Two-Way Family Favourites*, with the very excellent Judith Chalmers, and

BFPO 40, forging closer links with our boys on the Rhine? Course, he'd walked straight past me and was up on the eighth floor by the time I'd finished. How very like the man, I remarked to that Sue MacGregor who had just entered the foyer. She pretended to ignore me and walked straight into the lift. Salt of the earth.

Won't beat about the bush. Arrived home to find Brenda, my good lady wife, getting Sunday

Our 'Belling Roadster', bought out of 100,000 Kensitas coupons.

The good lady wife.

lunch ready. Roast beef, Yorkshire pudding, and all the trimmings. Brenda puts the sprouts on to boil on the Wednesday, we like them well done, otherwise she is troubled with wind. Just as we were about to start said dinner, Wayne, our youngest, stands up bold as brass if you please and says he's just decided to reject the whole concept of bourgeois patriarchal capitalist society, so he won't be wanting his oxtail thank you very much. Kids! I wish I'd never bought him that subscription to the *People's Friend* now, it's turned his head. How dare you, I said, how dare you talk to your father like that. It's time I told you a few home truths. For a start-off, money doesn't grow on trees I said, and you're never too old for me to take my belt to you, and I said, I said, I wasn't born yesterday, and I said, respect for your elders and betters wouldn't go amiss, and I said,

you're as young as you feel, and I said a stitch in time saves nine and I said fly me to the moon and let me play among the stars and I said many a mickle makes a muckle. And I was just about to tell him another home truth which I read in the *Reader's Digest*, when I happened to look up through my patio doors and saw a number of Eastern gentlemen of less than average height desporting themselves in traditional Japanese costume in the back garden. I told Brenda to keep the dinner in the oven and crossed the room, determined to give them one of my famous tongue sandwiches. But before I got there, their leader raised his ceremonial sword high above his head, uttered a scream the likes of which we don't expect down Warley way, and hurled himself through the windows, landing on my nylon tufted carpet in a shower of glass. His Oriental friends leapt in behind him, all with swords raised, and all with a most disagreeable glint in their Nipponese eyes. Brenda, I said, we'll never have enough dinner to go round, they'll have to go. But they didn't seem to want to go.

Will Harold Coaltart survive the invasion of Samurai warriors at dinnertime? Turn to p. 24 to find out.

4 VHF/FM 92·4-94·8 LW 200 kHz 1500 m

6.00am News Briefing

6.10 The Farming Week
Presented by Michael Pigstock.
Producer ALLAN WRIGHT *BBC Pebble Mill*

7.00 Today
Presented by **Peter Hobday** and **Sue MacGregor**
7.00, 8.00 Today's News Read by CLIVE ROSLIN
7.25 Sport with GARY RICHARDSON
7.30, 8.30 News Summary
7.40 Letter from France. **Alistair Cooke** gives more tips on how to use a condom.
8.40 The Week's Good Cause. This week **Benedict Spinoza** argues that God is the immanent cause of the Universe.
Editor JOLYON MONSON

9.00 News

9.05 Desert Island Stamps
Michael Parkinson invites another famous personality to 'lick your hinge' and discuss the eight postage stamps they would take with them to a desert island (they already have the Penny Black and Stanley Gibbons's Stamp Catalogue).

9.30 Breakaway
As usual, the BBC is paying **Bernard Falk** a small fortune for the inconvenience of staying in a 5-star hotel in Miami.
Producer JENNY MALLINSON DUFF

10.00 Loose Ends
Unravelled by **Ned Sherrin**, and a team of smarmy young gits who haven't got the big break into television yet.
Producer the nice MISTER GARDHOUSE

12.00 Money Box
For younger listeners. **Louise Botting's** daughter demonstrates how to slip a knife into the slot and get the 50p's out while mother is at Portland Place telling very rich people to put their money in offshore investments rather than into inner city redevelopment.

12.27pm I'm Sorry, We're not at all Funny
No scripts, no rehearsals, and here's the result. Half an hour of **Barry Cryer** laughing too loudly, **Humphrey Lyttelton** sounding embarrassed, and a claustrophobic studio audience becoming hysterical.
Producer PAUL SPENCER (stereo)

1.00 News

1.10 Any Questions
A right-wing bastard, a left-wing very rich journalist, a Captain of Industry who just happens to be a right-wing bastard, and a token female TV personality who, would you believe it, is a right-wing bastard as well.
(*Broadcast yesterday*)

2.00 You the Jewry
A weekly debate about Zionism, international finance, the Palestinian Problem, and Chicken Soup, introduced by a nice young Jewish boy who's a doctor already.
Producer NICK UTECHIN

2.50 Pottery Please
Our resident studio potter will throw a selection of ceramic artefacts requested by listeners. Presented by **Anne Stevenson**
Producer MARGARET BRADLEY
BBC Bristol

3.00 Bookshelf
Nigel Forde's guest this week is Barry Bucknell, who demonstrates how to make a strong and economical bookshelf for your own books out of all those large hardback review copies that publishers give out free to presenters.
Producer NIGEL ACHESON

3.30 Feeback
Christopher Dunkley, of the *Financial Times*, airs your complaints about BBC programmes, and asks offending broadcasters to return their pay cheques.
Producer MARINA SALANDY-BROWN
(*Re-broadcast next Sunday*)

3.45 Enquire Within
Listeners are invited to write in with their esoteric queries about obscure words. Presenter **Dilly Barlow** will then ask her researcher to look up the word in the Oxford English Dictionary and she will read out what it says.
Producer CATHY DRYSDALE

8.30 Law Inaction
Presenter **John Eidinow** looks at the lighter side of prolonged imprisonment without trial.
Producer ANTHONY MONCRIEFF

9.00 The Saturday Serial
Monadologie by G.W. LEIBNIZ
Starring **The Nolan Sisters** as the Monads.
Part 7, in which Leibniz criticises Descartes' mechanical conception of the universe, and Descartes ridicules Leibniz for wearing flared trousers. While searching his room, for a lost cufflink, he discovers the infinitesimal calculus at the very back of a drawer.
Leibniz................EDWARD DE SOUZA
Descartes................JOAN CAMPION
Directed by Philip Martin (stereo)

10.30 Even Looser Ends
In which the team of smarmy young gits still haven't made it into TV, and gratefully receive their repeat fees. (Repeat of this morning's broadcast).

11.30 Weak Ending
With **Bill Wallis, David Tate, Sally Grace** and **Jon Glover**
Half an hour of topical sketches, with tired, feeble punchlines, written by 147 people who presumably must all have day jobs.
Producer DAN PATTERSON

12.00 News

12.15 School's Night-Time Broadcasting
Ken Blakeson introduces 'What the hell do you think you're doing up at this hour, it's past midnight. Get to bed this instant'.
GEOFFREY SHERLOCK (E)

PHILOLOGICAL RUMINATIONS ON ASPECTS OF LIBERTARIANISM

This morning, on his return from the island of Crete, Donald Trefusis, Regius Professor of Philology at the University of Cambridge and extraordinary fellow of St Matthew's College, turns his waspish attention to the political storm arising from the appointment of the new Chairman of the Governors of the BBC. Dictated to his amanuensis Stephen Fry.

WASPISH? What do you mean waspish? Really, these boys who do the announcing have the most peculiar ideas. Waspish indeed. Hello. As most of you will already have read in this quarter's edition of the *Neue Philologische Abteilung,* that noble *vade mecum* of the linguistically concerned, my excavations into the origins and splendour of the Minoan dialects of Ancient Greek have just been completed, and have been compared in their size, scope and sweep to those more material digs made by Sir Arthur Evans at Knossos. Just some of the reviews of my work: 'A job of daring reconstruction and imaginative revivification,' *Language Today;* 'Professor Trefusis has cast a new light on Greek particles and their antecedents,' *Which Philologist;* 'I shall never look at the iotal slide in the same way,' *Sparham Deanery Monthly Incorporating the Booton and Brandiston Parish Magazine.* But my work has earned as much condemnation as praise. 'Left wing nonsense', writes Ferdinand Scruton in *The Times.* Of that I say little. I may only observe that the chain I wear about my neck

as I speak has depended from it a medal of the Elevtherian Order First Class, a token of appreciation from the Cretan people worth more to me than all the academic plaudits that I have no doubt will be mine before the sycamores have quite shed their last golden leaves on to the fast flowing waters of the Cam. Ah yes, to be home in russet England is something indeed.

Crete is a wine to be sipped with pleasure only for short periods. Without, it must be said, the steadying influence of the BBC's World Service to keep a rein upon my reason, my stay on that incomparable island would, I make no doubt, have been insupportable. The despatch of news, information, music, drama and imbecility from Bush House to Kalathas was unending and inspiring. But one oft-repeated theme on the short wave commentaries never failed to catch my attention. Imagine my horror to learn of the presentation of a dramatic series on the television in England while I was away, called, I believe, *The Molecule Mountaineer,* by a Mr Alec Bleasdale. Unless

I vastly mistake the matter a dramatist has distorted history to suit his own vile political ends. My grandfather happened to be at Etapes on the fateful three days in question and there is no question but that what has since been described as a revolution was merely an incident in which a private hesitated for a fraction of a second before carrying out an order to shoot himself. So great was the discipline, loyalty and affection for their officers of the British fighting man during that glorious war that this trivial act of hesitancy seemed like gross insubordination beside the norm of instant obeisance and respect that prevailed amongst the cheerful eager-to-be-senselessly-slaughtered soldiers at the Front: a small blemish that marred the beautiful truth of the Tommy's constant patriotic wish to obey in all things the noble, wise and strategically brilliant officers who led him. And now some ghastly playwright has tried to make something more of it than that. The government has rightly stepped in to intervene. My prayers are with the new Chairman of the BBC. His first duty, as I see it, must be to burn all tapes of, and prohibit any future productions of, the twisted plays of that arch propagandist and historical liar William Shakespeare. For too long have the radical lunatics running the television centre got away with encouraging such pseudologous, canting and doctrinaire mendacities as *The Tragical History of King John, King Richard III, Kings Henry IV, V and VI* in all their false and lying parts. As any historian will tell you, there was no hawthorn bush at the battle of Bosworth Field under which Richard III's crown did or did not roll. He never said, it is my duty to inform you all, 'My horse, my horse, my kingdom for a horse'. Shakespeare MADE IT UP. IT WAS A LIE, a dreadful, propagandist lie to please the fashionable place-servers of the day. I trust Mr Marmalade Butty will prohibit all performances of this frightful bearded playwright's works in future. 'Why', as the great predecessor in my Chair at Cambridge was used to ask, 'why are all the clever people left wing?'

Some of the more sensitive amongst you will detect a note of teasing irony in my voice. Of course you are right. Really it is beginning to look as if I cannot turn my back on Britain for a moment without ghastly interfering ignorant imbeciles meddling in things they quite simply do not understand. The idea of a politician being able to tell the difference between history and fiction is ghastly, they cannot tell a drama from a jar of pickled walnuts or a work of art from a moist lemon-scented cleansing square (such as Olympic airlines very thoughtfully provide for one's facial laving after an in-flight supper); the thought that they can be trusted to do so is absurd, preposterous and hideous. Fiction, it appears I must tell stupid people everywhere, is pretend, rather like politics. If every fiction masquerading as fact, whether it be revoltingly jingoistic or never so crassly iconoclastic, were to be anathematised, then it is not only copies of Shakespeare and Milton and Dickens and Joyce and Shaw that would be flung on the pyre but every recorded utterance by every human being. For as a philologist I am in a position to tell you that language is a lie. Yes! Language itself. A stone is a stone, the word 'stone' is not a stone, it is a token, a linguistic banknote that we exchange to indicate the idea of a stone. It saves us the trouble of having to haul one out of the ground to show our interlocutor what we mean.

Whether the assemblage of fatuity, prejudice, hatred and fear that constitutes the British public (those not listening at the moment) and the instruments of its political will understand the economics that regulate the supply and exchange of those linguistic banknotes or not—and fellow linguists will forgive my rather mechanistic pre-T.E. Hume approach—is immaterial.

Oh, gentlemen, ladies, all—the lies, the futility, the unreason, the folly. If you want repression, censorship, hypocritical moralising and propaganda on your televisions then go and live in America. There! I'm tired now, my thighs and hams are taut from the flight from Iraklion, I must visit my buttock masseur at Addenbrooke's: a splendid man—he leaves no stern untoned. If you have been, goodnight.

DEEP AND FRUITY VOICE: Radio 4. (*Long pause*). Well, in a moment, Ned Sherrin will be at the starting post all set to pace us through 55 minutes of conversation at a gallop! (*slight, self satisfied chuckle*). Then, at 11 o'clock, our 30-minute theatre production is called, *Drill Right Here Nurseypoos*. Amanda, a rather scatty but comic middle-class housewife — just up the Radio 4 housewife's cup of tea, you know — suddenly has an urge to become the weatherperson on the Ugandan Television Service. Her husband, Desmond, a long-suffering thoroughly nice and appealing comic neurosurgeon suddenly sees the 'red mist', returns home after a busy day's trepanning, and shoots Amanda's head off leaving it hanging by a single sinew. That's 30-minute theatre, and it takes us to 12 o'clock and our consumer programme *Up Your Drawers*. Today, the signature tune will be the same as ever, a dreadful jolly number recorded by the radiophonic workshop in 1967 and going — 'bong dee diddle dee bong' — and a boring young man in a suit talking about how much fluoride is in the average sausage and people in the street being asked inane questions and giving equally inane answers and someone from *Which?* magazine saying that the rubber sealing rings around the mixer could kill and then the man in the suit saying 'Bye for now and remember ... watch yourself. Then, at 12.30, our panel game invented by Edward J Shryan in 1955 called *It's Only a Game*, where a lot of old thespians get together, answer questions on Arthur Askey which they've got from the producer who was in the Green Room, but mostly they say 'Darling' and talk about 'dear sweet Noel', and laugh loudly. If you can hear it through all the wheezing, *The World at 1* is at the new time of 2.13, and then, at 3 o'clock, *Woman's Hour*, and here's Glevis Poocal to tell us all about it:

LONG PAUSE AS A TAPE IS BEING PUT ON BUT THE TAPE IS NEVER PLAYED:

That's *Woman's Hour* at a quarter past 2 this morning. Then at 4 o'clock, we go *Through Your Village* with Bribby Fatso. This week, Bribby visits South Ockendon's crematorium and sees how the bones are crushed in large sort of tumble driers with giant metal balls in, and he meets a man who connects the handle of his video tape recorder to his electricity socket for security reasons and accidentally kills himself twice a week ... (etc.)

21

Life in the Radio 4 Continuity Suite

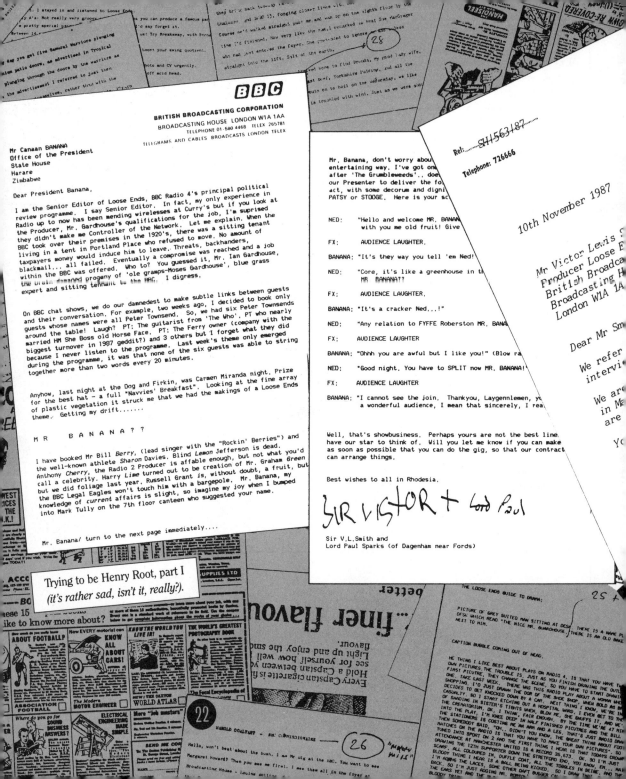

BBC

BRITISH BROADCASTING CORPORATION

BROADCASTING HOUSE LONDON W1A 1AA
TELEPHONE 01-580 4468 TELEX 265781
TELEGRAMS AND CABLES BROADCASTS LONDON TELEX

Mr Canaan BANANA
Office of the President
State House
Harare
Zimbabwe

Dear President Banana,

I am the Senior Editor of Loose Ends, BBC Radio 4's principal political review programme. I say Senior Editor. In fact, my only experience in Radio up to now has been mending wirelesses at Curry's but if you look at the Producer, Mr. Gardhouse's qualifications for the job, I'm suprised they didn't make me Controller of the Network. Let me explain. When the BBC took over their premises in the 1920's, there was a sitting tenant living in a tent in Portland Place who refused to move. No amount of taxpayers money would induce him to leave. Threats, backhanders, blackmail... all failed. Eventually a compromise was reached and a job within the BBC was offered. Who to? You guessed it, Mr. Ian Gardhouse, the brain damaged progeny of 'ole gramps-Moses Gardhouse', blue grass expert and sitting tennant to the BBC, I digress.

On BBC chat shows, we do our damnedest to make subtle links between guests and their conversation. For example, two weeks ago, I decided to book only guests whose names were all Peter Townsend. So, we had six Peter Townsends around the table! Laugh? PT: The guitarist from 'The Who'. PT who nearly married HM She Boss old Horse Face. PT: The Ferry owner (company with the biggest turnover in 1987 geddit?) and 3 others but I forget what they did because I never listen to the programme. Last week's theme only emerged during the programme, it was that none of the six guests was able to string together more than two words every 20 minutes.

Anyhow, last night at the Dog and Firkin, was Carmen Miranda night. Prize for the best hat - a full 'Navvies' Breakfast". Looking at the fine array of plastic vegetation it struck me that we had the makings of a Loose Ends theme. Getting my drift.......

M R   B A N A N A ? ?

I have booked Mr Bill *Berry*, (lead singer with the "Rockin' Berries") and the well-known athlete *Sharon Davies*. Blind *Lemon Jefferson* is dead. Anthony *Cherry*, the Radio 2 Producer is affable enough, but not what you'd call a celebrity. Harry *Lime* turned out to be creation of Mr. Graham *Green* but we did foliage last year. Russell Grant *is*, without doubt, a fruit, but the BBC Legal Eagles won't touch him with a bargepole. Mr. Banana, my knowledge of *current* affairs is slight, so imagine my joy when I bumped into Mark Tully on the 7th floor canteen who suggested your name.

Mr. Banana/ turn to the next page immediately....

Mr. Banana, don't worry abou[t]
entertaining way, I've got on[e]
after 'The Grumbleweeds'.. doe[s]
our Presenter to deliver the fo[llowing]
act, with some decorum and digni[ty]
PATSY or STOOGE. Here is your sc[ript]

NED: "Hello and welcome MR. BANAN[A]
           with you me old fruit! Give [...]

FX: AUDIENCE LAUGHTER.

BANANA: "It's they way you tell 'em Ned!

NED: "Core, it's like a greenhouse in t[...]
           MR BANANA??

FX: AUDIENCE LAUGHTER.

BANANA: "It's a cracker Ned...!"

NED: "Any relation to FYFFE Roberston MR. BANA[NA]

FX: AUDIENCE LAUGHTER

BANANA: "Ohhh you are awful but I like you!" (Blow ra[...]

NED: "Good night. You have to SPLIT now MR. BANANA!

FX: AUDIENCE LAUGHTER

BANANA: "I cannot see the join. Thankyou, Laygennlemen, y[ou are]
           a wonderful audience, I mean that sincerely, I rea[lly...]

Well, that's showbusiness. Perhaps yours are not the best line[s]
have our star to think of. Will you let me know if you can make [...]
as soon as possible that you can do the gig, so that our contract[...]
can arrange things.

Best wishes to all in Rhodesia.

SIR VICTOR + Lord Paul

Sir V.L.Smith and
Lord Paul Sparks (of Dagenham near Fords)

Ref:........SH/563/87

Telephone: 726666

10th November 1987

Mr Victor Lewis S[mith]
Producer Loose E[nds]
British Broadca[sting]
Broadcasting H[ouse]
London W1A 1A[A]

Dear Mr Sm[ith]

We refer [...]
intervi[ew...]

We are [...]
in Ma[...]
are [...]

Y[ours...]

Trying to be Henry Root, part I
(it's rather sad, isn't it, really?).

22

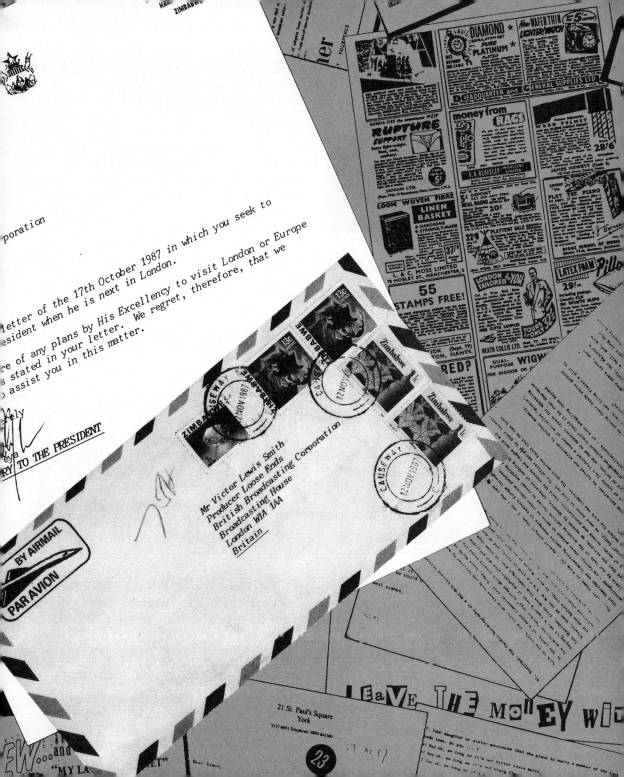

PART II

in which Harold
Coaltart, BBC
Commissionaire,
opts for sheer nylon
over fishnet

I am sorry. But it's not every day you get five Samurai warriors plunging through your brand new aluminium patio doors, as advertised in *Tropical Fish Digest Weekly*. Not the plunging through the doors by the warriors as advertised, you understand, the advertisement I referred to just then concerned itself with the patio doors themselves, rather than with the inscrutable and, may I say, not well brought up Oriental tykehounds. P'raps I'm old-fashioned. You may remember that, to our surprise, the 6th division of the Osaka Paramilitary Kamikazi Boy Scout Troop had been in our neighbour, Mr Sippi's garden shed, unnoticed, since 1942, although I have to say that I'd always wondered how the Co-op managed to sell seven shelvesful of *miso* soup a day when they can't even get shot of an outer of custard creams before the sell-by date.

Anyway, cut a long story short, I said to them ... I said HOW DARE YOU, how dare you jump through my aluminium patio doors ... they don't grow on trees you know. I tell you this, would you behave like that in your own homes? NO YOU WOULD NOT, and I'll tell you this, my good sirs ... you come over here, without so much as a by or leave, believe you me we'll have nothing Japanese in the house. As far as I'm concerned, I said, it's not that easy to forget things. My wife Brenda, I said, was in a

Japanese camp during the war. LOOK AT HER FACE ... course, to be fair, that's got nothing to do with the Japanese. Anyway, suddenly one of the Eastern ne'er-do-wells stepped forward with a very large pointed weapon, and shouted, in not very good English, the phrase DEATH TO WESTERN IMPERIALIST DEVILS. I said, I've never heard the likes, I said, how dare you. Back to your restaurants immediately. Well, cut a long story short, one of them whipped out his machete and in one stroke severed the cat's head from the rest of the cat.

Well, you could have knocked me down with a feather, or at any rate a small hammer. They don't mess about, these Japanese. Very good with their hands ... we have nothing but Japanese in the house. Anyway, quick as a flash, I said to Brenda, I said Brenda, there's only one way to get out of this alive. Go and get some sellotape, or similar unbranded adhesive tape, now! Anyway, cut a long story short, while the five of them were being distracted by our excellent oil painting from Boots of the *Laughing Cavalier* (much better than the original, no horrible rough nobbly surface), Brenda returned from the kitchenette with the sellotape. Straight away we put it to good use, making ourselves look slitty-eyed, as His Royal Highness so amusingly put it recently, slitty, slitty, slitty, slitty-eyed. I couldn't see a thing and I don't know how they can. Seeing us now as wisely Oriental gentlepersons like themselves, they apologised and left, using the sellotape to restore the cat to a state of near health, though I have to admit, nobody in the family has felt anywhere near like stroking a head hanging by a single ligament. But, as I always say, you can't make an omelette without breaking eggs, and anyway, many a mickle makes a muckle. In fact, I read in last month's *Reader's Digest* that it takes exactly 14 mickles to make a muckle ... and mickles don't

Mr Sippi, in better health.

grow on trees you know. Talking of trees, you won't guess what but, next morning, as we was woken up by the Teasmade, I glanced out of the window and what should I blimmin well see but Mr Sippi himself (who claims to be some sort of film reviewer), stiff as a board, up his pear tree dressed in nothing but a low cut, what Brenda described as a saucy lurex number, strapless ballroom gown with matching accessories.

Well, I said, it's disgusting. It lowers the tone of the neighbourhood, and Brenda agreed, and said she wouldn't be seen dead in a pair of

(e) Shoe 8/6. 17/- the pair.

patent leather shoes that colour. Unfortunately Mr Sippi *would* be seen dead in said shoes, on account of the fact that he *was* dead. Apparently, one of the Japanese warriors had introduced Mr Sippi to some rather exotic, not to say unsavoury ... but there you are I've said it, unsavoury Eastern peccadillos. I said to Brenda, I said, you shouldn't have peccadillos running all around the garden like that, least of all Eastern ones, I said, and I bet he's not cleared it with the Quarantine authorities. They're known to spread disease, which is, I said, why he's now the LATE Mr Sippi.

Anyway, I was just having a quiet chuckle at how the Lord our God, the Father, Son and Holy Ghost, bangs to right those who enjoy themselves in unnatural ways, and was considering asking John Waite to call by and demand that Mr Sippi Face the Facts, when Brenda turns to me, bold as brass, white as a sheet, and says ... Harold, she says ... I've just remembered. What Moggy? I say, what have you just remembered? She says to me, she says, I just remembered. Last week I fed Mr Sippi's peccadillos over the garden fence off our dinner plates. I said you what, woman ... you did what? Did you wash them up after in hand-hot water enriched with suds from a well-known brand of liquid that cleans more plates per penny than any other as advertised on the telly by Nanette Newman, I said? No, she came back with, I let the peccadillos lick the plates clean. Lovely pink rasping tongues they've got.

Oh ... tongues. Tongues is it? Do you know what you've done girl? You've only infected the entire family with deadly peccadillo disease. I said cancel the milk, we'll all be dead by lunchtime.

Will the Coaltart dynasty be wiped out by Mr Sippi's peccadillos? Turn to p.40 to find out.

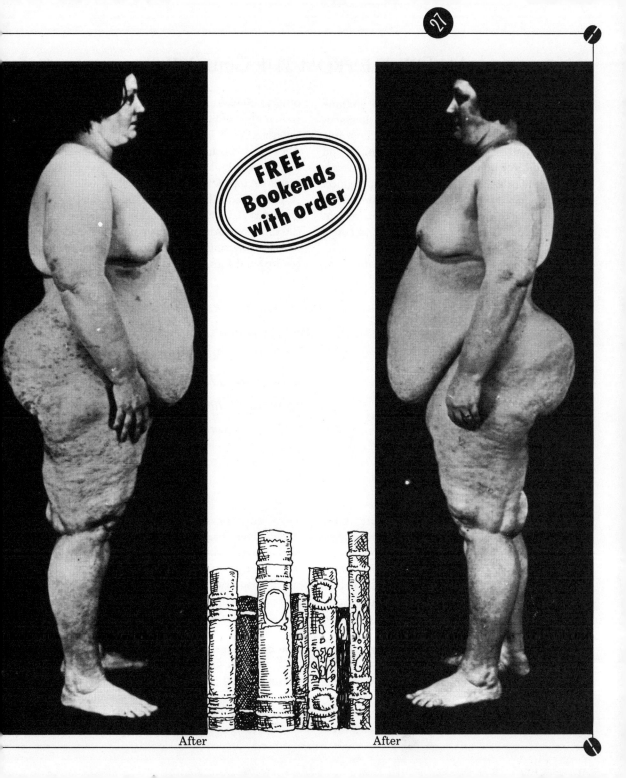

FREE
Bookends
with order

After   After

AN EPISTLE FROM THE COLONIES

YES, WELL, hello to you all back home. To think of you all folded in England's green bosom, thousands of miles away, while I am here in this thrusting virile forest of concrete and glass baffles my mind and threatens to unseat my reason. I find it hard to obey the instructions of the very kind young sound engineer and speak in a normal, level, tone of voice. If I am shouting, I apologise, but it is as much excitement that causes me do so, as the feeling that you are a whole Atlantic away from me.

I am here, as those of you who read the *Neue*

others who have not visited this island conurbation is that the buildings here are very tall. Oh yes. Enormously tall. Simply very very high. This is a fact. They just go up and up. Even as I speak I am on the 21st floor of a building, and still not yet a third of the way to the top. When examining Persian palimpsests of the Cyprian dynasty on the *sixth* floor of the University Library in Cambridge I was wont to succumb to spasms, so you can imagine the painful and embarrassing scenes and remonstrations that resulted in the lift when I first essayed this building.

DONALD TREFUSIS Emeritus Professor of Philology and fellow of St Matthew's College, Cambridge, is in America at the moment. He has sent back some of his impressions of a country he is visiting for the first time, dictated to his amanuensis Stephen Fry.

Philologische Abteilung will be aware, for a conference on the migration of the forward labial, here at Columbia University, New York. Without getting too technical it concerns itself with the influence of the Hispanic plosive on American English, a field in which I have been counted something of a specialist.

As this is the first time in my entire life that I have been outside Cambridge, you can imagine that I have suffered something of a fright over the past few days. Culture shock is, I believe, the terminus technicus employed over here to describe the massive sense of derangement and abstraction one feels. I can hardly believe that a whole other planet could afford as many surprises as this taut, urgent city. The first thing to tell

I have vertiginous seizures just thinking about it. This extraordinary height of the buildings informs the skyline, as you will readily imagine. The result, really most surprisingly, is one of astonishing beauty. I must also tell you that the taximeter cabriolets, or taxi cabs as they call them for short, are coloured a gay and vivid yellow, not unlike a spring mimosa, that lends a seasonable splash of primrose to the place. I assume that they change colour throughout the year, red for autumn, white for winter and perhaps a cerulean blue for summer. Ah, no, the young engineer on the other side of the glass partition here is shaking his head. Clearly yellow is a settled thing.

Now, to my speciality. They say 'specialty' here. The

iotal elision, as we philologists call it, is not uncommon. They also drop the final letter 'i' from aluminium and deliver the word as aluminum. And who is to say them nay? One of the commonest subjects for discussion here is stress. It is talked about all the time. They appear to have established a causal relationship between stress and diet, which is very fascinating to me. I must say I am enchanted and encouraged with America's interest in my discipline, in England most people seem not to consider philology or linguistics from one day to the next. But stress is certainly a talking point here. Take, for instance, Hong Kong. They say *Hong* Kong, which always seems to imply that there is another kind of Kong which they are anxious not to confuse with that of the Hong variety. *Hong* Kong. The stress on the first word. There is a proprietary blend of instant coffee here called Maxwell House. At least that's what we would call it. Maxwell House. Here it is called *Maxwell* House. A much less even stress. They somehow believe, though, if I am to believe the newspapers, that this stress problem is caused by smoking and lack of exercise as much as anything else. I had always understood that it was simply a result of the transhistorically separate development of British and American English. I have a great deal yet to learn. A gentleman approached me in the street earlier and asked 'Have you got a light mac?' to which I replied, truthfully, 'No, but I've got a dark brown overcoat.' The reward for this candour was a bloodied nose. I think I am going to have to study the customs very much more closely before I dare venture out on to the streets again, alone. Thank you for listening. If Mrs Miggs is tuning in, as she promised she would, 'Don't forget to dust the books, Mrs M, and remember that Milton's worming tablets are on the tantalus beneath the Cotman etching in the study. You have to hold him down on his back and prize his jaws open to get them in. You may take next Tuesday off.' Goodbye everyone.

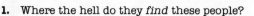
MAT COWARD'S TEN MOST FREQUENTLY ASKED LISTENERS' QUESTIONS ABOUT RADIO 4 CHAT SHOWS

1. Where the hell do they *find* these people?

2. Why the hell don't they leave them there?

3. How do you make *Loose Ends* so amazingly wacky and risqué?

4. Is it true that Libby Purves is a man, or was that just the *News of the World* getting carried away?

5. You don't seriously expect me to believe that that was just the *News of the World* getting carried away?

6. Why oh why doesn't somebody *please Stop The Week*?

7. Purely as a matter of historical interest, has *Start The Week* ever had anything interesting on it?

8. Are there any plans to make *Midweek* three times as long? Only, my passport's out of date.

9. Why isn't *Loose Ends* called something with 'week' in it? Are they snobs, or did they just forget?

10. Why do all chat shows consist entirely of people plugging books, records, films, leaks, etc? It's a disgrace. I've written a book about what a disgrace it is, perhaps you'd like me to come on and talk about it?

11. I don't suppose you poofs have got so much as a Grade 4 CSE in Maths between the lot of you, eh?

THE ONE MOST FREQUENTLY ASKED PRODUCER'S QUESTION ABOUT RADIO 4 CHAT SHOWS

1. How are we going to fill an hour again this week?

How a Loose Ends piece is made

VLS I often get letters from fans asking me how I manage to produce my ratings-saving masterpieces each week for *Loose Ends*. So, I've recorded a week in the life of a *Loose Ends* artiste. I spent a week with me, following me everywhere, and capturing my every creative move. The piece starts at the very moment the previous week's piece finished.

FX NED WINDS UP PROGRAMME. OFF AIR, MEMBERS OF PROGRAMME CONGRATULATE THEMSELVES: 'WONDERFUL' 'MARVELLOUS' 'SOOPER DARLINGS'.

VLS Bastards. It's Saturday morning and what you're hearing is a rare recording of a post-*Loose Ends* back-slapping session, where BBC producers and presenters reassure themselves with: 'I was wonderful, how were you?', 'Did I mention the book title often enough?', 'Super darlings', 'More champagne, loves', 'The goat was splendid', and 'do come to number ten and meet Mummy sometime.'

FX NED: 'DID YOU GET A SONY AWARD, A SONY AWARD, A SONY AWARD?'

VLS Course, it's all very fine and dandy for that lot in London playing at being the Bloomsbury Group. Just because I've got chronic halitosis, I'm exiled to this upgraded phonebooth at Radio York. I wouldn't mind, but they're so understaffed here that I have to read their dreadful local news, while the local team are knocking back the falling-down water at the George.

FX RADIO PRODUCER? YORKSHIRE ACCENT: 'ER...WOULD YOU READ THE NEWS PLEASE?'

VLS See what I mean?

FX RADIO YORK NEWS JINGLE.

VLS Here is the local news. There has been a *very* serious spillage of sugar at Tesco's in Wiggington. Police have not yet named the woman who dropped the bag near the detergent counter. And more news is coming in of that faulty telephone box in Haxby Road. Reports suggest that a 10p piece has been wedged in the slot with a lolly-stick... Oh, this is ridiculous, I'm going home.

FX FOOTSTEPS.

VLS Every week I pass the Commissionaire who salutes me, and wishes me well...

FX COMMISSIONAIRE, YORKSHIRE ACCENT: 'YOU WERE BLOODY CRAP THIS MORNING, SONNY.'

VLS ... and out through the main entrance, where once again I fight off the York *paparazzi*.

FX WHIRR OF ROLEX CAMERAS. CAMP VOICE: 'HOLD IT', 'COULD YOU LOOK HERE PLEASE MR LEWIS SMITH, JUST HERE PLEASE'.

VLS *Tropical Fish Digest* press me for quotes on my supposed love triangle with Molly Sugden and Idi Amin. I say nothing, smile enigmatically and step into the cockpit of my Sinclair C5. I live three miles away, so, with a good wind behind me, I arrive back on Sunday evening in good time for Thora Hird, and a passionate kissing session with my pet whippet.

FX SONGS OF PRAISE, KISSING. CUT TO RICHARD CLAYDERMAN, PIANO.

VLS Sunday evening is something of a ritual with me: Richard Clayderman, a bath, a cup of Horlicks, and a good book. This week I'm reading Camus, and I rub the pages all over my face because Camus keeps my skin young-looking. Anyway, after that Mrs Tribley, my concierge, comes over and affords me a complete colonic irrigation with two quarts of warm soapy water. There's a lot of *Loose Ends* creative work to be done and *mens sana in corpore sano,* as my old granny used to say.

FX   PHONE RINGS.
VLS   That'll be Idi.
FX   LIFTS UP PHONE. IDI: 'WHAT'S ALL DIS ABOUT DE MOLLY SUGDEN?'
VLS   It's Idi, speaking from his Saudi Arabian hideout. Life's not easy being General Amin's toyboy. I slip into my Tom and Jerry pyjamas, and don my clip-on hairy chest given free with last week's *Bunty* comic, and it's off to bed. It's a playboy flat, so naturally we're talking black nylon sheets, and a full-length mirror on the ceiling. Unfortunately it's a single bed, but the mirror comes in handy when I need to practise my semaphore.
FX   IDI STILL ON PHONE: 'SHE BAD WOMAN, VERY VERY BAD WOMAN'.
VLS   *(yawns)* Monday morning, and I'm gently woken up...
FX   ALARM CLOCK ELECTRONIC BLEEP.
VLS   ...by my Goblin Ginsmaid.
FX   BLEEP STOPS, STEAM HISSES
VLS   It's the deluxe version that adds the tonic, slices the lemons automatically and switches on the television.
FX   CLICK. NEIGHBOURS THEME TUNE. VLS SINGS ALONG, NONE TOO WELL.
VLS   I sing along with the television, and open my post. The producer of *Loose Ends,* the nice Mr Gardhouse, has mailed the theme for next week's programme. It is 'Six People Who Have Got a Book Out, and are Desperate to Plug it,' and the regulars are Mat Coward, who I think is crap, Stephen Fry, who's not only crap but toffee-nosed, though I notice not too toffee-nosed to do peppermint ads on the telly, Craig Charles, who thinks he's the people's poet, but he's crap too, and the usual mélange of token cockneys or upper-class twits.
FX   PHONE RINGS.
VLS   Oh no, that'll be Mr Gardhouse. I'd better zap *Neighbours* and slip into something more cultural.

FX   NEIGHBOURS STOPS. GREGORIAN CHANT BEGINS. LIFTS RECEIVER.
VLS   Hello Mr Gardhouse... Yes, it's a Gregorian chant actually, I always play it at this time in the morning... Oh, do you think it's cultural then?... Well, you know, it puts me in touch with the old Muse...Ah, no ideas *as yet* for a piece, Mr G, I tell you what, give me a bell this time Thursday, I'll definitely have something for you then...Right then, well I'll just fade out slowly to give the impression that time is passing...Right, just fading out now...
FX   FADE TO SILENCE.
       NEIGHBOURS. VLS SINGS ALONG. HE HAS NOT IMPROVED SINCE MONDAY.
VLS   By Thursday afternoon, things are really hotting up. Down under Raylene has run off with Joylene, while her sister Vosene has had an affair with Noylene, and Roylene has witnessed Raylene taking an overdose of kerosene and is going to kill Violene with Iodine.
FX   LISTENS TO *NEIGHBOURS*. REPEATS SOME OF DIALOGUE.
VLS   You can stick your Shakespeare, give me *Neighbours* any day. But there's work to do; another edition of *Neighbours* to catch up on, then I really must start on my *Loose Ends* piece.
FX   CUT. TYPEWRITER TYPES VERY SLOWLY, VLS HUMS *NEIGHBOURS*.
VLS   It's Friday now, and I've got this week's theme sorted out. As my fans know, many of my Sony Award winning pieces are reviews of Phone-In Services, where I record people without them knowing and then cut the tape in such a way that I sound very clever while they sound like imbeciles. It's a living. Anyway, as you can hear by my furious typing, I've got my theme. But things can go wrong. I decided to give the new Medical Phone-In Service a thorough going-over, starting with this one, the Premature Ejaculation Line.
FX   PHONE RINGS, TAPE PLAYS 'WELCOME TO THE HEALTH CALL DIRECTORY, YOUR GUIDE TO MEDICAL INFORMATION. THIS TAPE IS ABOUT PREMATURE EJACULATION.' PHONE CLICKS OFF, DIALLING TONE.

VLS Anyway, that was rubbish. It was all over in a second. Then I tried the Circumcision Line, but I got cut off. Then I tried the Tinnitus Line, but it just rang and rang and rang. The Diarrhoea Line was engaged all day, I tried Amnesia Line but I kept forgetting the number, and anyway, the piece was banned by the BBC even before I thought of it, so it left me with one option really.

FX *NEIGHBOURS* THEME. CLINKING OF BOTTLES AND GLASSES.

VLS It's Friday night and things are looking bleak. No *Neighbours* until Monday morning, and no *Loose Ends* piece. Until.....

FX PHONE RINGS.

VLS Ah, that'll be my big break on the phone.

FX ANSWERS PHONE.

VLS Hello...what's that you say? David Bowie, Frank Sinatra *and* Molly Sugden in York together?...And what's that you said, even though there wasn't enough time in that last pause for you to have said anything at all?...And you say they'll only give an exclusive interview avec moi?...And you say that this whole routine is starting to sound like one of those contrived Mat Coward sketches?...Really?...And what's that you say about why do I keep repeating everything you say?...Oh, he's put the phone down.

FX RECEIVER GOES DOWN.

VLS And that, Ned, is how radio is made. So, now for that interview they'll all be talking about, Bowie, Sinatra, and Molly Sug... Oh dear, we seem to have run out of time. Oh well, I'll sell the transcript to *Jackie* magazine. Back to you, Neddy baby, and can I have my money now please?

We asked famous people what they think of *Loose Ends*...

The Chief Rabbi: 'I'm generally pretty busy of a Saturday morning, unfortunately, but my two teenagers, Rachel, 14, and Zak, 16, assure me that Lice Nurds is "the hottest groove in radioville, oldster". '

Malcolm X: 'I love it, man, I just love it.'

Idi Amin : 'Satire is very much my "bag", and this show's got the lot.'

Controller, Radio 4: 'Oh is that one of ours? I'm more a Third Programme cove, m'self. Still, jolly good, carry on.'

Clare Short MP: 'I'm usually in the supermarket at that time on a Saturday, but I'm told it's dreadfully funny.'

Lord Carrington: 'Never quite caught it myself, sorry, but at NATO HQ the younger element talk of little else. What d'you say you call it again? Ah yes, that's it. *Down Your Way* was always my favourite.'

Keith Best: 'We all listen to it at home ... and at home ... and at home ...'

Raisa Gorbachev: 'What a far-out diggit show! Me and the better half dig swinging to it all the crazy time! Wanna buy a Levi?'

Desi Arnaz Jr: 'Count me in guys! Let's go-go-go!'

Princess Fergie: 'I like big hot ones. Hahahahahhaha!'

MAT COWARD

A post mortem charity appeal

Hello. Tonight, if you're still listening, I want to stir the conscience of our nation by appealing to you in a few simple words on behalf of a few simple people. As you know there have been over the years many issues in this country which have given rise to deep public sympathy: the slave trade, the ten hours bill, the fate of the battery hen, Home Rule for the TUC and so on, so it is with confidence that I appeal to you over a cause which I am sure is of the gravest concern to us all. I speak of the work of the General Post Office. Never in the history of human endeavour has so much anxiety been caused by so few to so many. And this hasn't been easy. Frustration is extremely hard to organise on a national scale — it takes years of specialised training, scientific advance and, above all, millions of pounds must be spent.

Let's get the facts straight. Few of us are aware of how the problems are actually created. Basically by sending letters. However pleasant these are to receive, they just make life more difficult for the postman. Verbal diarrhoea has become a national disease but we must fight it together because it all falls into the hands of the postman. Putting it bluntly, he has to shift the stuff. Now the average letter weighs half an ounce. Multiply that many, many times and add it to the weight of the average parcel, multiply it again and you have a hernia. We are all too ignorant of the suffering we cause.

There is the postman getting up at 4.00 a.m., leaping on to his bicycle at ten minutes past, getting up again and fiddling with myriads of tiny keys, rushing to and fro, sorting, re-sorting, delivering, redelivering and, most important of all, working out the delays. Now these are complex and many people are unaware of the enormous cost involved. Some of your mail chosen at random, though obviously including anything marked 'Special Delivery', catches, say, first post on a Friday morning. It is then carefully stored at Head Office until it can be sorted last thing on Tuesday. It travels half way round the country, perhaps visiting some of the most famous beauty spots in these islands and then back to you. It is scribbled on, re-addressed and finally put in a brown bag at Head Office, Newcastle-under-Lyme. Could you do all that for 18p ? Of course you couldn't. Neither can the GPO, so further price increases have been scheduled for the New Year.

Sophisticated computers ensure that mistakes are not just left to chance, and to co-ordinate our appeal we have given it a covering title: CHAOS. Complete Hash Of All Services. Not, as some have unkindly suggested, Continually Having A One-day Strike. We are confident that CHAOS will arouse strong feelings and keep pace with British Telecom's recent campaign UNOBTAINABLE (Utter Nerk Operating British Telephones And Irish Numbers Are Best Left Ex-directory). Some of you will also be familiar with Postman's Knock. This is no longer true. They will try and force even the bulkiest package through the hole in your door.

Now I don't want you to think that I'm merely appealing for money but, since we've mentioned it, all cheques should be made out to the Post Office and sent to this address, which I am not going to tell you about since we are concerned to receive the money. Instead, we suggest a monthly banker's order as being the most convenient method of transferring things from one place to another.

And remember: 'Get the most from your Post' — use Araldite, thick twine or small digital padlocks as appropriate.

BY PAUL BURBRIDGE

SHERINE ENTERPRISES

☆ THE LOOSE

Some variant of Monopoly or Snakes and Ladders, I suppose; if I could think of a truly original one I'd market it for £20:99 at Hamley's instead of putting it on two pages of a book. Anyway, it'll include the following: counters for playing with, shaped like Ned, the nice Mr Gardhouse, etc; squares marked with: **'Epilepsy cured'** (Miss a Turn), **'Met Stephen Sondheim in a lift'** (Win the Game) **'Arrange lucrative book contract'** (Go to 'Advance') **'Announce on air that Jeffrey Archer has a spotty back'** (Go to Jail).

The game will be some sort of promotion affair. Whenever your counter gets one square behind someone else's you play your 'knife in the back' card and they go back to being secretaries. Promotion is got in various ways; I keep thinking of sexual ones at present.

What about **'Friends and Enemas'**? Or a series of forfeit squares; **Enema** (take a strong purgative etc). Or odd squares with. **'Hotel on Park Lane'** (wrong game, miss a go), **'Head of Radio says you are maturing'** (buy grey suit and throw again), **'Head of Radio says your work is hackneyed'** (miss a go and buy a kaftan and flared trousers) **'Get job writing Ned's ad libs'** (disappear into total obscurity).

BROADCAST LIVE ON RADIO 4

THE 1989 SONY RADIO AWARDS

Presented by

The Rt. Hon. Mr. Pussycat Willum MP (DSO and BAR) pictured above, stark naked

Mr. Yakamisho Sittogossa Yit. Chairman of Sony UK

SPECIAL CATEGORIES

The Douglas Bader Award for Best Use of Synchronised Swimming on a Single Edition of *The Financial World Tonight*
Presented by Bonnie Langford

The Arthur Mullard Award for Upholding the Highest Standards of Received Pronunciation on Local Radio
Presented by Jack Ashley MP

The Lourdes/LondonRubber Company for the unlucky Local Radio Presenter who has to hire an oversized DJ from Moss Bross, you know where the collar sticks up so that you know it's hired, and then go down to London to receive some bit of horrible plastic on stage from Judith Chalmers, while enduring patronising applause from the 'big boys' in network radio, as you say 'a big thanks to the entire production team of *Live From Wigan*', and then after the ceremony the 'big boys' come and tell you how important they think local radio is and they snigger and snort into their glass of G and T and a microsecond after the handshake they turn away and forget you for the rest of their lives Award.
Presented by Brian Tampax

The Jonathan Miller Award for the Radio 3 Announcer who can cram the words: 'THRENODY', 'POINTILLISTIC', 'KLANGFARBENMELODIE', 'DODEDCAPHONIC', 'POST MODERNIST' and the phrase 'RICHLY WOVEN FINELY HONED TEXTURES' into a single sentence.
Presented by Frank Bruno

'Happy feet. I got d'ose happy feet...'

THE *LOOSE ENDS* 'BEING THERE' KIT PART ONE

THE CUT OUT 'N' KEEP
DRESS YOUR OWN
NED SHERRIN DOLL

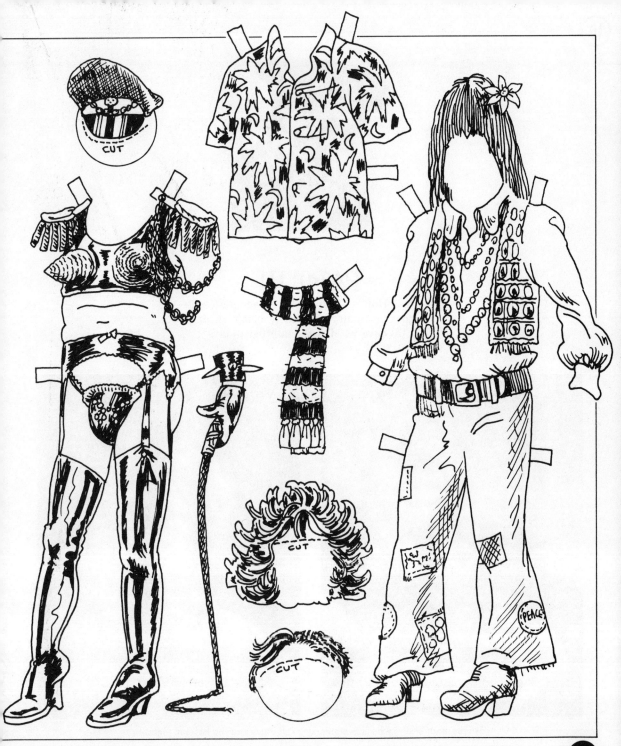

CUT

CUT

CUT

PEACE

PART III

in which Harold Coaltart, BBC Commissionaire,
enjoys the luxury afforded by double glazing
(as advertised by the late Ted Moult)

'Wayne' and 'Tracy', who subsequently go off on a camping holiday together.

I won't beat about the bush. When a man is about to meet his maker, his mind becomes concentrated on the higher things of life. With only twelve minutes left to live, I decided to play some of the tracks I'd never got round to listening to on my *Reader's Digest* 50 Box Set of the hits of James Last. Funny how he never gets into the charts, when he's had all those hit records. My children, Wayne and Tracy, fought against time to finish off some crocheting which my good lady wife insisted was for posterity. I said to her, I said you know as well as I do that Mr Posterity left the street weeks ago. You're obsessed by the man. He didn't want to know you then, and since you've only got eight minutes left to live, the chances of a flourishing romance are slim to say the least. Suddenly it struck me. We took the *Reader's Digest* up on their attractive offer of an 18-piece

Sippi, as you remember, was now in a state of severe decomposition, and I said it's disgusting ... I'm going to contact the Brentwood and Ongar Health Authorities and get him buried. It shouldn't be allowed ... it lowers the whole tone of the neighbourhood, having a brazen, half-rotten corpse dressed in a low-cut lurex frock hanging from a fruit tree. S'pose we had visitors. Right, I said, I'm putting my foot down, I AM PUTTING MY FOOT DOWN. And with that, I put my foot down, then the other one, and stormed out of the house, straight down the shopping precinct to get myself kitted out for Mr Sippi's funeral. First stop, the tailor for a black suit. You've got to do things properly, and despite Mr Sippi's perversion he *was* for the burners and he *was* a neighbour. Blood's thicker than water. Actually it's exactly 1.6 times thicker than water, it's amazing what

Mr Sippi, in worse health.

Willow Pattern gorgeous Tupperware Service. Plastic, but durable and very useful for stop-offs on the hard shoulder, flask of tea, cheese sandwiches, and all the trimmings, very handy when the Little Chef looks to be full of the lower orders ... I think you know what I mean. Rough trade. Nuff said.

Anyway, cut a long story short, nothing lives on Tupperware, including harmful microbes, so we were saved, and I said one day girl, I said, we'll look back at this and laugh. Anyway, Mr

you learn from the pages of the *Reader's Digest*.

Anyway, I arrives at the tailors and bold as f'ing well brass, up comes the manager and says would I like to buy a suit off the peg. I say yes, and he says Mr Peg, there's a gentleman here wants to buy a suit off you. Well, it turns out that Mr Peg deals in shot silk only, and each suit costs at least three quarters of a million pounds. Course, in that position, I had to buy one to save face, but frankly, it's the last time I shop at the Army and Navy. He said to me, he said, there you are Sir, it fits like a glove. And you know he was right. There were five pouches over my head and an enormous opening at one end. I said to him, I said it's disgusting. I said when I pay three quarters of a million pounds for a suit, I expect to receive a suit, and not a blimmin 6-foot glove. I said this establishment is run by cretins, and he came back with some nonsense about how the Cretins got bought out. I said, I remember Solly Cretin, he was a PROUD man, and a bespoke tailor to the gentry and the good burghers of Warley and its environs. People bespoke highly of him, I said, you'd never get him selling a shoddy suit that looked like a glove. They shall hear of this in the *You and Yours* office. Anyway I bought it because he told me I'd grow into it, and so the next step was off to the chemist's for some embalming fluid on special offer this week.

Having bought said fluid I found myself returning to the shop no fewer than 16,000 times that afternoon, and making excuses by buying trivial items such as 20,000 nasal hair clippers. But for some reason I was strangely attracted to the assistant who frankly was as ugly as sin, stout, and of a certain age, and with a face which, to be fair, did have two ears, two eyes, a nose and a mouth, but not necessarily where you'd expect. Then suddenly, as I proposed marriage, it struck me. 'Excuse me,' I said 'but are you wearing pheramones?' I said ... 'because I can't think why I should be so aroused by you.' Suddenly, realising that her secret had been discovered, she took revenge action, by whipping out an electric cattle prod from under the Home Brew counter, connecting it to a nine-million volt battery from the electrical section, and holding it half an inch from my temples, if you don't mind.

Will Harold Coaltart escape retribution at the hands of the woman from the Embalming Counter? Turn to p.60 to find out.

Linda Leigh fancy-weave rayon dress in Dusky-Beige with matching embroidery. Slim line skirt, straight in front, gored in back, with subtle waist pleats and twin hip pockets. Sizes: 24,26,28,30 only.
See chart on p.5.
State size.
G1657...Each 93/6

BBC SOUND EFFECTS INDEX

Macaws
Calls of blue and yellow macaws with other màcaws and hill mynahs
in background. (Somerset) – Jan 73 – 6'36"
Macaw being garotted. (From 78 disc) – 1934 – 8"

NH32A(s)   b
EC1106H   b04

Machete
See Para-Military Organisations: Women's Institute. Also mastectomy

Machine Guns
MG 42 (nickname Spandau) machine-gun, Bren gun, small arms fire, World War II
(From 78 disc). Rec. Netherlands. – 1945 – 3'1"

EC500X   f01

EC7F9(s)   f01
EC1106H   b03

Mackerel
Mating call of male mackerel – Apr 67 – 2'46"
Mackerel being garotted. (From 78 disc) – 1934 – 8"

Mafia
Refer to Dir. Gen.

EC102A   b01
EC102A   b02
EC1106H   f14

Maidenhead
Traffic on Maidenhead bypass, rush hour – Jan 82 – 2'42"
Traffic on Maidenhead bypass, night – Jan 82 – 1'36
Maidenhead being ruptured. (From 78 disc) – 1933 –8"

NH113Z   f07

Mallard
Mallards alighting (East Anglia) – Sep 57 – 1'0"
Mallard partially garotted, escaping, being caught again, wings stapled behind back,
then garotted. (From 78 disc) – 1943 – 3'08"

EC1106H   b05

EC83G   f03

Mallet
Hammering wooden stake into vampire with mallet – Aug 87 – 1'53"
Hammering sirloin steak into vampire with mallet (specially created effect) – July 87 –
58'45"

EC89G,H,I,J,K,L

Mamba
Extremely poisonous African tree snake partially garotted, sound engineer slumping
forward, recording equipment collapsing. (From 78 disc) – 1934 – 8"

EC1106H   b06

EC199A   f03
EC199A   f04

Masseur
Masseur receiving £10, providing massage – May 87 – 1'34"
Masseur receiving 4 x £10 notes, providing full massage with 'extras' – May 87 – 3'45"

EC2S16(s)   b04
EC1106H   f09

Mastectomy
N.H.S. mastectomy in operating theatre – Dec 65 – 9'35"
Mastectomy "done private" with machete (From 78 disc) – 1933 – 8"

Maturbation
See also Self-Abuse

EC44A   f01
EC44A   f04

Masturbation.
Female masturbating with vibrator (with multiple orgasm) – Nov 83 – 3'07"
Female peasant masturbating with carrot (single orgasam, Calabria) – Nov 83 – 2'46"
Female Catholic masturbating with crucifix, orgasm, cry of 'Mother of Mary, I have sinned'
(Dublin) – Aug 83 – 4'01"
Male masturbating and freeze-framing on video machine – Nov 83 – 2'48"
Male, premature ejaculator, masturbating – Nov 83 – 4"

EC44A   f03
EC44A   b01
EC44A   b02

Meadowlarks
Song from a Western Meadowlark. (South West Oregon)
– May 72 – 2'11"

NH45A   f03

LISTEN WITH MURDER

by Paul Burbridge who, though not actually a bona
fide *Loose Ends* contributor, listens quite often.
Well...once... because he was in the bath when
Breakaway ended and he didn't want to get out
because it was cold...you know what it's like... well,
actually, it's a fair cop, he's never really listened to
the programme at all, but we met him on a bus
yesterday and he had this sketch which had just been
rejected by the *Tropical Fish Digest*...

ANNOUNCER: Hello everyone. Lesson number twelve. This is a pane of glass. Very smooth, very clear and *very* fragile. If I take a sturdy instrument such as this piece of lead pipe and go like that...

FX: PANE OF GLASS SHATTERING

...well, you can hear the result. This, on the other hand, is a human skull. If I give it the same treatment but this time with a wooden instrument, such as a lump of four by four, we get a different sound..

FX: CRACK OF WOOD HITTING HEAD

...Hollower, isn't it? More resonant. This resonance can be sustained by first covering the skull with something protective and blue; for instance a policeman's helmet, and the sound will change again. Listen.

FX: BASH ON POLICEMAN'S HELMET
And again... **BASH** ...Again... **BASH** And stop! **BASH**

Good. Remember the sounds we learnt last week? The machete into the white cabbage..

FX: CABBAGE CHOPPED IN HALF

...and the machete into the base of the neck.

FX: CABBAGE CHOPPED IN HALF

An identical sound wasn't it? But this week I want us to listen to the sound of another popular instrument, the boot. Sometimes it can sound like this..

FX: SLAMMING OF CAR BOOT

...or like this

FX: FOOTBALL KICKED INTO TOUCH

...or even like this..

FX: ONE THOUSAND JACKBOOTS MARCHING TOWARDS MICROPHONE

But this one has a slight difference. I wonder if you can spot it?

FX: KICK IN THE STOMACH, FOLLOWED BY SHARP GROAN

Did you hear that? Here it is again...

FX: KICK, GROAN

Notice how one sound follows another, showing how easily they can be worked into a sequence...

Head to nose **CRUNK!,** Boot to head **DUMPFF!,** Wood to glass **TWANGTERSPLINKLE!** Fist to stomach **KERRDNGUNG!,** Chain to neck **THWAPPSLIT!,** Bottle to head **TASSHHSCHHLOKK!.**

So now let's put all the sounds we've learnt so far back into their original composition with full choral backing...See if you can recognise the piece..

FX: CROWD OF FOOTBALL SUPPORTERS FIGHTING THREE HOURS BEFORE KICKOFF

Not too difficult, was it? That was, of course, the famous Saturday Afternoon Fever theme from the great Sporting Requiem by the composer Mentalli de Fichente.

DONALD TREFUSIS is still on his lecture tour of the universities and women's institutes of England. This week has seen him in Newcastle, Exeter, Norwich, Lincoln and, tonight, Nottingham. On his way between Norwich and Lincoln he had time to talk to his old pupil Stephen Fry, whose parallel comedic tour has attracted widespread concern.

DR TREFUSIS EXPOSTULATES ON HIS REVOLUTIONARY NEW PRINCIPLES OF EDUCATION

Dictated to his amanuensis Stephen Fry

HUGELY SO TO YOU ALL. Firstly I would like to thank the obliging undergraduate of the School of Mauritian Studies at the University of East Anglia in Norwich who so kindly retrieved my valise last night. I am sorry he had to look into it in order to discover its rightful owner, and I assure him the sum required in used bank-notes will be left at the assigned place. I look forward to the safe return of the appliances.

Now, I'm particularly glad I caught you this just now because I wanted very much to have a word about this business of education. I have visited so many schools, universities and polytechnics in this last week, listened to the tearful wails of so many pupils, students and teachers that I feel I should speak out. As one who has spent his entire life, man, boy and raving old dotard, in and out of educational establishments I am the last person to offer any useful advice about them. Better leave that to politicians with no education, sense or commitment. They at least can bring an empty mind to the problem. However I would like to alienate you as much as possible at this time by offering this little canapé from the savoury tray of my experience. If you would like to kill me — and you would not be alone in that ambition — forget poison, expunge strangulation from your mind, and entirely fail to consider the possibility of sawing through the brake cables of my Wolseley, there is a much simpler course open to you. Simply creep upon me when I am least expecting it and whisper the phrase 'parent power' into my ear. Stand back and admire the effect. Clubbing cardiac arrest. Parent power; schmarent power, I say. Don't misunderstand me, oh good heavens remove yourselves as far as possible from the position of not understanding me. Democracy and I have no

quarrel. But on this head if on no other believe me, parent power and democracy are as closely related as Mike Gatting and the Queen Mother, and unless someone has been keeping a very fruity scandal from me, that is not very closely at all. Parent power is not a sign of democracy, it is a sign of barbarism. We are to regard education as a service industry, like a laundry, parents are the customers, teachers the washers, children the dirty linen. The customer is always right. Oh dear, oh dear oh dear. And what in the name of boiling hell do parents know about education? How many educated people are there in the world? I could name seventeen or eighteen.

Because of course education is not the issue. 'Heaven preserve us from educated people,' is the cry. Ask Norman Tebbitt, for whom a leering naked teenager in a newspaper is no different from a Titian nude, ask him what education means. Ask the illiterate ghouls of Fleet Street or Wapping Street or whatever unfortunate thoroughfare they now infest what education is. A poem with swear words has to be banned from television or they will squeal for weeks. They've dealt with the socialists in the town halls, now they want to turn on those clever people who mock them in their plays and books.

This new England we have invented for ourselves is not interested at all in education. It is only interested in training, both material and spiritual. Education means freedom, it means ideas, it means truth. Training is what you do to a pear tree when you pleach it and prune it to grow against a wall. Training is what you give an airline pilot or a computer operator or a barrister or a radio producer. Education is what you give children to enable them to be free from the prejudices and moral bankruptcies of their elders. And freedom is no part of the programme of today's legislators. Freedom to buy shares, medical treatment or council houses certainly, freedom to *buy* anything you please. But freedom to think, to change? Heavens no. The day a child of mine comes home from school and reveals that he or she has been taught something that I agree with is the day I take that child away from school.

Teach Victorian values, teach the values of decency and value and patriotism and religion, is the cry. Those are the very values that led to this foul century of war, oppression, cruelty, tyranny, slaughter and hypocrisy. It was the permissive society it is so horribly fashionable to denounce that forced America to back out of the Vietnam War, it is this new hideously impermissive society that is threatening to engulf us in another. I choose the word 'engulf' with great care. Look at those Islamic cultures in the gulf for moral certainty, for laws against sexual openness, for capital punishment and flogging, for a firm belief in God, for patriotism and a strong belief in the family. What a model for us all. Heaven help us, when will we realise that we know nothing, nothing. We are ignorant, savagely, hopelessly ignorant — what we think we know is palpable nonsense. How can we dare to presume to teach our children the very same half-baked, bigoted trash that litters our own imperfect minds? At least give them a chance, a faint, feeble glimmering *chance* of being better than us. Is that so very much to ask? Apparently it is.

Well, I'm old and smelly and peculiar and I've no doubt everything I said is nonsense. Let's burn all those novels with naughty ideas and naughty words in them, let's teach children that Churchill won the Second World War, that the Empire was a good thing, that simple words for simple physical acts are wicked and that teenage girls pointing their breasts at you out of newspapers are harmless fun. Let's run down the arts departments of universities, let's string criminals up, let's do it all now, for the sooner we all go up in a ball of flame, the better.

Oh dear, listening back I can't help feeling that some of you may have got the impression that ... well, it's only because I care. I do care so very much. And when I'm away from home and see how poor and ignorant a people we are, well it upsets me. I think I should take one of my slow release capsules and perhaps snuggle up with an Elmore Leonard and a warming posset. If you have been, I wonder why.

BRITISH BROAD
BROADCASTING
TELE
TELEGRAMS AND CAB

FILE

M. Pierre Boulez
IRCAM
31, rue St. Merri
75004
PARIS
FRANCE

Dear M. Boulez,

There is a current trend at the BBC where my friend Lord Sparks and I are both producers, towards complete eradication of all signature tunes. Only the "Archers" and the very excellent "Money Box" (presented by Louise Botting) remain. The Controller is a tone-deaf madman. I'm sorry, but these things have to be said.

You're a rebel. I'm a rebel, M.Boulez, I require a sig tune for my programme "Loose Ends", and your name was passed onto me by Sir Michael Tippett who unfortunately declined my generous offer. Says he has an opera to finish. Sounded like the old heave ho or the vieux coup de grâceas you say on your side of la manche. Never mind, he's finished with the BBC from now on. He yesterday's man sig tune wise.

Here's what I'd like. Something catchy. But please don't use a drum machine. When you hear the tune, you should say to yourself.. "ah.. that's a nice tune, it must mean one thing and one thing only... that Loose Ends is about to start. I really must settle down with a cup of Horlicks and give this programme my undivded attention". Can you come up with the goods Mr. Boulez?

Look. I went to the Q.E.H last week and heard something by you, I think it was called Pli Selon Pli? Frankly, I think you should sue the performers. They were all over the place. So much so, that you couldn't hear the bloody tune at all. I'd have walked out if I'd been you. In fact, I did. Even though I wasn't you. I guarantee that the Doris and Arthur Twinkle Eastbourne Amateur Palm Court Orchestra (who we use regularly) are crack sight readers, as long as you don't venture into more than two sharps, or put the time signature in something silly like 3/4. And complex compound duples are RIGHT OUT of the question until Mr. Twode gets his glasses sorted. It's all sticking plaster with him. We want tunes and more tunes. OK. £50 (that's 500FF in Frog) receipt of ms. No more to be said.

yovrs, VLSmith and paul

Sir Victor Lewis Smith and Lord Paul Sparks (Of Dagenham near Fords),
PS: Have you thought of teaming up with your sister Patti, as Donny and
Marie Osmond did in the 70's.

Mr. Victor Lewis Smith
BBC
Room 7076
Broadcasting House
London W1A 1AA

date: 17th November 1987
vos réf:
nos réf:
objet:

Dear Mr. Smith,

Mr. Boulez has asked me to reply to your kind letter.
Unfortunately, he is so busy these days that he simply
won't have the time to write something for you, however
brief it be. Believe me, it is not a question of money.

'Pli selon pli' is indeed a very difficult piece to play
and it has happened to Mr. Boulez that the results were not
always is he would have liked them to be, especially if he
did not dispose of enough rehearsal time. As for performances
conducted by other conductors, he cannot really say as he
has not heard many.

Sorry about the signature tune.

Yours sincerely,

Astrid Schirmer
Secretary to Pierre Boulez

IRCAM
Institut de Recherche et Coordination
Acoustique/Musique

Centre Georges-Pompidou
Centre National d'Art et de Culture

Téléphone (1) 42.77.12.33

Mrs Tribly
Very Luxurious Penthouse Flat
York

Dear Simon Scott,

RE: MRS TRIBLY'S COMPLEAT AND GENTLEWOMAN'S GUIDE TO REVENGE THOROUGH

Mr Lewis Smith for whom I concierge to said you was desperate for any materials to publish in association with Mr Hearst apropos the Loose Ends programme on BBC Home Service.

I originally submitted this manuscript to 'Amputee Love' magazine, a specialist medical journal with the eyes blacked out, but they said it was 'not for us'. I then contacted the Siberian Correspondent for 'Pravda', a newspaper printed in foreign, who said it did not align itself sufficiently closely with its Marxist-Leninist doctrine, and suggested, anyway, that it should have more pictures. It was him what suggested after reading your name on a lavatory wall in Brest Litovsk that I send it to you he said it reminded him of 'Mrs Beeton before mid-life change and Ebury are a soft touch', to quote the socialist tykehound's own words.

I enclose some sample pages. Other topics I have covered are:

The Church of England, Freemasons (and, for the men) Women Who Fake Orgasm, Wholefood Shops, Crippled People, Archbishops, Women Who Don't Fake Orgasm, Drunks on Trains, Papal Nuncios, Computer Bores, Scientologists, People With Ghetto-blasters, Bad Trad Jazz Bands With People Who Chant 'Ooo ya ooo ya' During Drum Breaks, G & S Societies, Women Who Breast Feed in Public, Epileptics, Buskers Who Play Streets of London Out of Tune Accompanied by a Pre-recorded Cassette, People Who Play the Crumhorn, Steve Race, Alternative Comics, Foreign People, People Who Wear Bow-ties, People Who Pick Their Armpits and Have Wives Called Rona, Bankmanagers, Estate Agents, Esther Rantzen, Mormons, Monty Modlyn, The BBC, Doctors, Garage Repair Men Who Say 'It's scrap' at 4 am on the M63, Bespoke Tailors, Jesus Christ, Arabs Buying 15 Grm Tins of Truffles in Fortnum and Mason's, Animal Liberation (give them a hammer and chisel and a tortoise and ask them to liberate it from its shell), Academics With Leather Armpatches and Halitosis, Australians, Harold Smart... the end, as they say, is listless.

Enclosed, is my publicity picture. Yes, it's an old one, and flattering, but what the fuck. So long as it doesn't cause a murder. I want 10%. Let's make the baby fly.

Mrs Tribly

Mrs Tribly

AMATEUR DRAMATIC SOCIETIES

Have brought much pain into the world, but you can't blame them for that. The hard wooden seats used in the average church hall precluding sweet slumber. The only solution is to take briefly to the stage yourself, and finish the play with a few well-chosen words. I once took an hour and a quarter off the Chipperfield Players' production of *Waiting for Godot* by

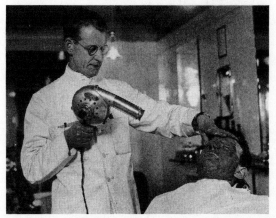

Cutain call, Mr Beckett.

strolling on set in a plastic mac, wellingtons and a crutch announcing 'sorry I'm late – still, now that I'm here you can all go home' and making a dignified exit. They tried to adlib their way out by claiming they were waiting for another man of the same name, but their hearts weren't really in it and we all got out well before closing time.

SEE ALSO: GILBERT AND SULLIVAN

ATTILA THE HUN

Is a man after my own heart. His light-hearted quip: 'It is not enough that I should succeed; everybody else must fail' never fails to bring a smile to my lips, and his invasion of Gaul in 451 A.D. was a real corker and has me in stitches.

SEE ALSO: VARNEY, Reg.

AIRLINES

I was recently indecently propositioned by a drunken Irish person in the lounge belonging to the very excellent Air India company. Fortunately, I had the time to slip into his luggage a very, very thin piece of tin foil, fashioned into the shape of a revolver. Through the complicated X-Ray machinery, the thin model looks, to all intents and purposes like a real gun. A real must.

Also, all too often one finds that the seat adjacent to one's own is being occupied by some brain-damaged working class oik. Rather than fuming silently, and dwelling on the many benefits of compulsory euthanasia, simply empty a bagful of tinned sweetcorn niblets (never go out without one) into a vomit bag during take off, when your neighbour's limited attention will doubtless be elsewhere, and then sit back. By the time the neighbour has had his seventeenth free Babycham, commence faked vomiting into the bag. After you've finished, glance down at the bag, say 'waste not want not', and spoon large dollops into your mouth. If there's another spare seat on the plane you should find yourself alone before too long.

SEE ALSO:
SANDERS, Colonel
and POPE, His
Holiness the.

'IT WORKED FOR ME!'
Says satisfied
customer Mrs. N. E.
Falkirk of Bolton.

BRITISH RAIL

I avenged myself on a particularly obstreperous ticket collector in the following manner. I arrived at Liverpool St Station, breathless, with only a few minutes before my train was due to depart, intending to purchase a ticket from the inspector on the train. However, the aforementioned collector refused adamantly to let me on. Ever smiling, I apologised to him and rushed to the ticket office (five flights of stairs up) where, fortunately, I was able to purchase a ticket quickly. I also bought a 5p platform ticket, and on returning, showed the latter to the collector. He was, of course, intensely suspicious thinking that I was a penniless 'Diddycoy' or gypsy type but the B.R. Rules obliged him to let me through warning me not to put one foot on the train. I stood on the platform until the train began to move then, quick as a flash, leapt on board. The collector immediately rushed down the platform blowing his whistle and shouting to his cronies to stop the train. He and two others eventually boarded my carriage and storming up the aisle he bellowed some indecent abuse. 'YOU!' he said, 'I told you... RIGHT...OFF THE TRAIN!!'. Innocently, I deftly removed my legitimate ticket from my top pocket and showed it to him. Crestfallen, he bowed his head and shambled off the train. Since the train had gone some distance it was
a) very amusing to see an old

gentleman negotiate the considerable drop from carriage to tracks and b) very amusing to watch him commence his ⁷/₈ths of a mile hike back to the station.

I am led to believe that he has since taken early retirement.

SEE ALSO: NUN ON A TRAIN, insulting a.

BICYCLE THIEVES

A certain flair for D.I.Y. is necessary for this one as you are unlikely to persuade a legitimate bicycle shop to help you. The diagram below should assist.

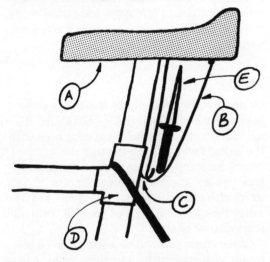

To the underneath of the cycle seat (A) attach a length of stout elastic (B) stretched over a small flange (C) protruding from the mainframe (D). Standing proud from the frame, directly beneath the seat (A), and above the flange (C), place a very very sharp knife (E), which may be tipped with curare as desired. Leave the bicycle in a prominent place (I find outside D.H.S.S. establishments work a treat), obtain a good vantage point for observation and enjoy.
N.B. Do not attempt to ride the bicycle yourself without first rendering it harmless by removing knife (E).

ELISHA

Like me, a man who enjoyed a bit of good honest fun. How's this for a sense of humour?

And he went up thence unto Beth-el:
and as he was going up by the way, there came forth little children out of the City,
and mocked him, and said unto him: Go up, thou bald head.
And he turned back, and looked on them, and cursed them
in the name of the LORD. And there came forth two she-bears out
of the wood, and tare forty and two children of them.

Kings I, ch.2, v.23-24

GUARD DOGS

We are a nation of animal lovers, and I have made love to as many animals as the next man, but it's only fair that a miscreant pooch be brought to book. I enjoy the following morsel of canine fun, a harsh but fair rebuke to any over-zealous watch-dog.

RECIPE
Take 500g (1.1lb) raw meat, and dice. Cut a watch spring into small pieces and sharpen ends. Bury a piece of spring into each chunk of meat. Then, toss the meat into the premises patrolled by the watchdog. Observe and, most of all with this cooking business... ENJOY!

INLAND REVENUE

It's not easy to gain financially by hoaxing these people, except possibly by faking death (returning all letters with 'moved, believed dead' scrawled on them will stall them, but is not a satisfactory long-term solution). For many years, when a tax man called at my luxury apartment, I would simply point to a patch of carrots in the garden and inform him that I had survived for years by eating the carrots, thus, nil expenditure. Whatever the nonce, a letter on the following lines will bring a glow of satisfaction, as one lies back and imagines a bevvy of scurrying secretaries, anxiously trying to locate previous correspondence:

YOUR ADDRESS
YOUR NAME.
(or other way round if preferred)

My ref: Malik/Spon.223f.

Sir,

Thank you for your letter of 14th. inst. I have since spoken to my accountant who informs me that your proposed reimbursement of £13,869.59p. is in accordance with his own. Therefore, if you would be good enough to send me your cheque by return of post, I shall consider the matter of my overpayment of tax closed.

Yours etc.

(What a tax person
looks like--)

LECTURERS – PARTICULARLY AT CONFERENCES

Schooldays may be far away (more's the pity I say!), but from time to time most of us more reasonable and middle-class members of society find ourselves having to attend conferences where some spotty, bearded little tinkle drones on and on. Simple one this.

If the blackboard is of the revolving calibre, simply sneak in before lessons and disconnect the loop. A harsh tug from 'Sir', and the whole 'board' whiplashes across the room. I don't doubt that there could even be a death. Or...

More spectacularly, why not slip a dozen or so 'Swan Vesta' match tops into the wedging in the blackboard rubber.

SEE ALSO: PIANO, injecting jelly through the keyhole of a.

MALAYSIANS

When saying goodbye to a Malaysian friend at the airport, why not slip a few small packets of heroin into his hand luggage. Just a few grams are sufficient, and how he'll laugh when he's frisked by the Malaysian customs men, especially since, in Malaysia, possession of any drug, no matter how small, means immediate hanging.

N.S.U.

Or non-specific urethritis to those of you who have never had to visit the 'special clinic'. It's not much fun, but as well as getting even with the bastard who put you through the experience, why not turn your misfortune to good use, for was it not the well-known songsmith and philosopher Helen Shapiro who sang: 'Pick yourself up, dust yourself down and start all over again'?

At the clinic, you will be asked for a list of recent sexual partners, and given forms to pass on to them (in some cases, the hospital authorities may even agree to do this themselves). YOUR list should include at least one Justice of the Peace, an M.P. and a handful of clergymen. Pop the form through their letterbox.

Leave the form (with your note face up) in a prominent place. Make photocopies. Leave them in fish and chip shops or where a churchwarden is likely to see them.

SEE ALSO: CHURCH OF ENGLAND, sueing the entire.

SPORTS CARS

Men with undersized penises often find it necessary to indulge in vulgar and showy display. Here is a fine way to deflate their egos. I've done this many times, and it never fails.

If you pass someone in their TR2 or somesuch sports car waiting for gasps of admiration, run up to them and say, 'Gosh, what an absolutely fanTASTIC car! You must be very proud of it. Isn't it a 4500 22 chassis? The (whatever it says on the front) is my favourite. I wish I had one.' After some more fawning comments enquire: 'Would you mind if I run home and get my camera? I only live round the corner and I'll be back in two minutes'. Then carry on with your shopping. Often, I've walked home an hour later, I see them still parked, the dimmer ones on whom the light has not yet dawned!

SEE ALSO: EXHAUST PIPE, whistles bunged up the.

PHONE-IN CHAT SHOW HOSTS

These egotistical 'jocks' are usually about as interesting as watching paint dry. What can be really effective, if you find one who is sporting a mid Atlantic accent, is to phone him and quiz him on matters U.S. Invariably, they'll know nothing about the place, and if you're very clever you can get them admitting that they come from Basildon or some such place. Put it to them straight: WHY THEN DO YOU HAVE AN AMERICAN ACCENT? Listen to the rounded R's ebb away as the programme continues.

I've also blocked an entire phone-in programme. It's simple but you may need help. If you have a switchboard with about 10 lines, then Robert is your Father's Brother! Most Radio Stations have only 7 or 8 lines. By telephoning the station and, as soon as the phone-in receptionist answers putting him on 'hold' you effectively put that line out of action.

It's a great ruse to gradually reduce working lines to just two, since the quality of calls becomes even worse than usual. The most tedious of callers start to get 20 minutes while engineers furiously attempt to sort the problem out. It's hopeless.

When you get to the last line, go on air and say to the 'jock' 'OK matey... you're on your own now!' Then sit back for comfort and safety and enjoy the ad-libbing skills of the host as he tries to fill the last 85 minutes of airtime with no callers. This ruse can be performed by getting several friends into telephone boxes.

SEE ALSO: HAYES, Brian.

Hi there. And we've got one helluva show for you this evening.

PROBLEMS

Sometimes you may have problems in various fields of experience. For example, a shop assistant may tell you that she does not stock your particular brand of shoe polish (as happened to me recently). Simply look her in the eye and say... 'Then there is no other alternative. I am going to call the police'. And leave the premises. It will ruin her day.

SHOPS

We are plagued, in this country, with unhelpful shop assistants. (See: PROBLEMS). However, here's a ruse which I've tried on several occasions to great effect.

Take 1 large piece of bloody liver, a red rubber glove filled with hardened plaster of paris, a £10 note and a large raincoat with deep pockets. One of the arms on the raincoat must be cut off.

If a shop assistant has been rude or vulgar to you, wait for about one month. Then prepare to make your return to the shop.

Fold your right arm behind your back so that you look 'armless'. Put your left hand in your pocket. Proceed to enter the shop. Ask for something very small and very fiddly, like, for example, 'Orange Pip' sweeties. These are perfect. Ask for them 'loose, please'. By now, the assistant will be tense.

At that very point, and with great drama, pull out your rubber glove hand. Stuck to it should be a £10 note. Mould the fingers so that access to the note is very tricky indeed so that the assistant has to fiddle a lot.

As the assistant pours the comestible into your 'hand' make sure that they fall to the ground, but thank her anyway. Ask her to put your change deeply into your pocket. At the bottom of your pocket you will have placed the raw liver. As soon as she feels it say: 'I'm so sorry, I have trouble with 'me waterworks''. She will almost certainly pass out.

TAXI DRIVERS

One usually has to endure the free expression of their fascist views. They are usually fat with double chins on the back of their necks, which can be particularly sick making especially at night time. However, a little revenge can be obtained, either by engaging them in a conversation of a medical nature, or by taking a friend with you into the back of the cab. I've done this many times, and only once have I been asked to leave.

Make it clear that you are a cardiac specialist at a London clinic. Drop a few 'intramuscular convulsions' or 'peripenetic palpitations' to set the scene. Then go on to describe a particularly nasty and fatal case brought in that day. Describe the patient, by giving an exact description of the taxi driver..... 'In his 40s.... overweight..... red faced... short back and sides... wore a grey sweater... did a lot of driving. Sat around all day. Sedentary. Never had any trouble before. Of course, we tried to operate, but when someone's in that condition, there's hardly any point. I told his wife. Useless. He was right as rain yesterday... and now... well, the widow was distraught I can tell you!' Stare hard into the driver's face while paying the fare. Nod your head sadly but say nothing.

Theydon Bois? Not at this bleedin' time of night, guv'nor. (A typical friendly London cabbie.)

The thing I like best about plays on Radio 4, is that you have to make your own pictures, the trouble is, just as you finish drawing the outline of the first picture, they change the scene, so you have to start drawing another one. Take last week. There was this radio play about a woman who went shopping. I'd just drawn the door of the shoe shop, when, bold as brass, she decides to get knocked down by a car. Next thing I know, we're in casualty. So I start etching out a hospital ward. I even get to the point of shading in sister's tights when, blow me, she snuffs it, and we're at the crematorium. Ok, I think, fair enough. By the time we're 47 minutes into the play, I'm knee deep in half-finished pictures and the bill from the stationers is costing me an arm and a leg. That's just radio drama. Then somebody said, 'Oh ... didn't you know, the great thing about football matches on the radio is that you have to make your own pictures'. So I tuned into *Sport on 2* and the first thing I hear is that today's crowd attendance at Manchester United is a record 35,673. Ok. So I'm just drawing the twelfth supporter down the Stretford end, you know, em ... rattle, scarf, all coloured in, duffle coat, all the toggles in beige, and the next bloody thing I hear is a ball being kicked. So I draw that, but just as I'm adding the laces, some other daft bugger called Brian Robson kicks it back. So I'm just adding Mr Robson's five o'clock shadow, not even finished the ears yet and the bloody ball somehow gets stuck in the net. Nets are bloody tricky things to draw, and I don't mind saying that without a ruler, I could have been there all night. Anyway, there's a backlog of 12,684 pictures to make and I haven't even started on *The Financial World Tonight* and it's making my nerves bad. It beats me why anybody ever even listens to the radio. It's supposed to be relaxing, but when you're getting deliveries of 60 gallon drums of paint every hour ... relaxing my foot.

THE NICE MR GARDHOUSE

PART IV

in which Harold Coaltart, BBC Commissionaire, says 'I know what you were burying in the garden last Thursday.'

Let's face it, it's not every day you find yourself cornered by a crazed fat old cow holding a thin prod with a lethal nine million volts surging through it. As she went in for the final lunge, frankly, I closed my eyes and prayed to the Lord. It's funny, but the one thought that flashed before my eyes was why isn't my life flashing before my eyes? Then I felt it make contact with my forehead and an overwhelming sensation of warmth flooded through my temples. Was I dead? Was this the afterlife? As I opened my eyes I focused on the incontinence section of the chemist's array, so it probably wasn't the afterlife, I reasoned, in that I've heard that people tend not to have trouble down below and round the back in the Hereafter. St Peter isn't known for being taken short and having to spend a penny while the likes of Che Guevara get through the gates. Anyway, cut a long story short, it would appear that I had mistaken the assistant's intention. She was not, we laughed later, wielding a lethal cattle prod at all. Oh no. What she was holding was a Boots battery-operated curling tong, a safe model, but now discontinued because it requires nine million volts just to reach room temperature. No, she said, all she was doing was trying to coiffure me a kiss curl, in the style of a certain Mr William Haley, a popular songster of the 1950s, who, she maintained, was the spitting image of me. Course, I made my excuses and left.

Tuesday found me commissioning in the foyer of Broadcasting House. Tuesday is a West Indian cleaner, a charming young lady though sadly not at all fair of face, which goes to show you shouldn't believe every old wives' tale you hear. Russell Harty passed through the lobby, and I detained him, quizzing him thusly: 'Why, Mr Harty, do you end every question with "is it not"?' I asked. 'That is my own business, is it not?' he replied, and took the lift. A couple of years in the army, if you catch my drift.

Wednesday saw us all heading off towards the crematorium for Mr Sippi's immolation. As I drove in through the main entrance I was handed what I thought was a rather unsavoury in-house monthly publication, sponsored by the Liqueur Manufacturers' Association. It was called, if you don't mind, *Crème de Menthe*, and claimed to be a guide to the best crematoria in Essex. I said to Brenda, I said it's disgusting, they have no respect at all. I said I remember a time when I would say I'll write a strongly worded letter to the Editor of the *Warley Gazette*, and she said, well why don't you then, and I said right I will say it then, I'm going to write a stiff letter, I said, a STIFF ... Unfortunately, just as I shouted the word STIFF, Mrs Sippi, already in deep shock because of the sudden revelation of her husband's little foibles apropos the women's clothing, heard the word STIFF and burst into floods of tears. We had to laugh ... Brenda and I both decided that it's much better than bottling these things up. Anyway, cut a long story short, before the ceremony started, I went to reclaim a brooch that I'd borrowed Mr Sippi last week and which, frankly, wasn't going to end up as molten plastic at those prices. There he was ... in his box, looking healthier than I'd seen him for years, with a peaceful and contented expression on his boat race, and wearing his favourite pink chiffon blouse. I didn't mess about, I don't mind telling you. I got straight in there and located the brooch which, for some strange reason, was under his left armpit.

Just as I was telling Mr Sippi's deaf ears that they'd done him proud with the brass handles and the nylon quilting fitted as standard, it suddenly got very dark and I realised with a dull flash that the lid of Mr Sippi's box had slammed shut. Well, if that's not enough, there I am making small talk with a rather lifeless ex-neighbour, thinking that my Wayne or Tracy would have the sense to locate my whereabouts when, suddenly, I hear the strains of 'Roses are Blooming in Picardie' from the organ, and the sound of a mechanical conveyer belt. With a jolt, Mr Sippi and I were heading for a better place, first stop, some pretty powerful burners.

Will Harold Coaltart enjoy the full warmth of the burners? Turn to p.80 to find out.

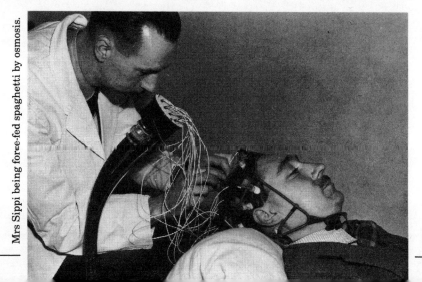

Mrs Sippi being force-fed spaghetti by osmosis.

Bert Weedon
Epperstone House
45 Penn Rd.,
Beaconsfield
Bucks

Dear Bert "Mr. Guitar" Weedon author of 'Play in a Day the Bert Weedon Way' which is a book I relished and studied and emulated as a teenager especially your duet arrangement of "When the Saints, Oh When the Saints, yeh When those Saints Go Marching In..". Great stuff.

I am not *exactly* the Producer of Loose Ends. I was a Producer, but it was more, your long range shipping forcast and your weeks good cause than your top rated zany chat shows. Frankly, I wouldn't give em time of day. But I did agree to appearing on the programme and now virtually run it with a rod of iron. Mr. Weedon, may I call you Bert, I am firm. Very firm. And I like the cut of your jib.

I was recently talking to Ravi Shankar who plays a type of Pakistani banjo, popularly known as the sitar, and I reminded him of your proud boast, announced by your good self on the popular children's television show "How" hosted by a matronly, fuller figured lady called Bunty, that you were capable of playing no fewer than 1,000 notes on your guitar in a single minute.

To my astonishment, Mr Shankar, on hearing this, *well* lost his rag(a), using such filthy language as the likes of which myself, as a Christian soul, could not bring myself to duplicate here. Mr Weedon, between ourselves, I suspect that Mr Shankar has a touch of the thugee in him. I tried to placate him with an anodyne Esther Rantzen-style pun about baby-sitars, but to no avail. "Tell Weedon I can play more notes in a minute than he ever can" ejaculated the trembling, thin-lipped Mr S. "Mr Shankar" I replied, jumping to your defence, "you are talking of the man who played solo guitar for the very first Milky-Bar-Kid commercial in 1957". "Pah, small fry" spat Ravi "even removing *all* thirteen sympathetic strings *and* some of the big ones, I shall still undo this Occidental running-dog with his Fender Stratocaster". "With or without mizrab?" I taunted him. "Without".

Bert. Will you take up the Loose Ends challenge? We'll leave it at that - the ball's in your court.

Yours sincerely,

V L Smith

V.L.Smith,
P.P.P.Sparks,

P.S. Tell me please, was it *really* you playing banjolele on the "Sarongster at the Palladium" commercial in autumn 1959?

Trying to be Henry Root, part III
(it's getting sadder still, isn't it?).

Bert Weedon

EPPERSTONE HOUSE · 45 PENN ROAD
BEACONSFIELD · BUCKS · HP9 2LN

Telephone: Beaconsfield (STD 04946) 2697

Dear Victor,

Thank you for your letter of the 29th October, and I found your idea very interesting. I would be delighted to take part in your programme if you can get it organised, and needless to say I would have lots of ideas and notes, plus anecdotes etc should you need them.

You are correct in thinking that I do endeavour to play the guitar faster than my fellow guitarists, and I often feature this in my act, asking the audience to time me. I have a great admiration for Ravi Shankar, and I think with all our mutual years of experience we would have a great deal to talk about.

Finally I enclose a photo brochure for the office as requested, and I hope that we might meet some time in the future.

With every good wish,

Yours sincerely,

Bert

BRITISH BROADCASTING
BROADCASTING HOUSE LONDON W1A 1AA
TELEPHONE 01-580 4468   TELEX 265781
TELEGRAMS AND CABLES BROADCASTS LONDON TELEX

Dear Mr. Shankar,

I was given your name by a Mr. Ragam, the waiter at my local Indian restaurant, the 'Manzil'. Do you know it? They do a very excellent Tikka, and I have a running joke with Mr. Ragam who, during my tikka, approaches me and says:

How is your tikka? And I reply:
Not bad, though I have had some palpitations recently.

This usually brings the house down, especially if the boys from the local rugby club are in. Anyway, recently, after a very violent fight there, as a result of one of the local props wanting that awful music they play jolly well turned off, your name came up. Mr Ragam assured me that you were pretty nimble when it comes to twanging an instrument he referred to as the Zitar. I am firm, very firm indeed.

I am hardly familiar with the Zitar. Indeed, string instruments and me don't see eye to eye, but I do remember once on the popular Southern Television children's programme, "HOW", Bunty interviewing one of your colleagues, a Mr. Bert Weedon. During that interview, Mr.Weedon claimed that he could play "1,000 notes per minute, Bunty".

Mr. Shankar, I wonder, can YOU play 1000 notes per minute?

I present on a programme called Loose Ends on BBC Radio 4, and my concierge, Mrs Tribly and myself thought it would be more than just a little fun to challenge you and Mr.Weedon to a duel.

Tell me, would you be willing to take up the SHANKAR/WEEDON zitar/guitar challenge which would be broadcast to over 2 million eager listeners. I MAY be asking Larry Adler to judge, but please do not raise your hopes too high. Please confirm this booking A.S.A.P. to the above address. I must inform you that I originally approached a Mr. Imran Khan rather than your very excellent self, but he informed me that fast bowling was more in his line. Frankly, I know one or two things about stringed instruments, and told him to watch out he didn't damage his fingers.

In the meantime, may I say that George Harrison must be proud to have you as one of his STAR, Third World Country pupils. What was it..? Tune a day? Go on, let us into the secret! OK?

SIR VICTOR ✝ Lord Paul

Yours faithfully,
Sir Victor Lewis Smith   and Lord Paul Spaarks (of Dagenham near Fords)
Room 7076 Broadcasting House. Letter reply only please.

Victor Lewis Smith
Producer Radio 4
BBC
Broadcasting House
London W1A 1AA

30 October 1987

Dear Victor

RAVI SHANKAR

Many thanks for your letter of October 20. - I don't have any
signed photographs in the office just now, but I'll ask him to
sign one for your son when he is next in London. What is your
son's name?

Ravi Shankar's diary is full for 1988 and most of 1989, and he
will still be in India in January, but I'll put the idea to him
in principle at the next opportunity.

All good wishes

Yours sincerely

Basil

Basil Douglas

*Our artist's impression
of Mr. Shankar's
baby sitar.*

Basil Douglas Artists' Management is the trading name of
BDMG Ltd
Directors Basil Douglas, Maureen Garnham
Registered in England No 1871312
Registered Office 2nd Floor, 88 Colleg
Employment Agencies Act 1973
VAT No 417 6262 53

Getting into television

'BUT TO YOU..... 624 LINES.OK'

VLS As you may remember, my most recent Sony Award was for Radio Personality Most Desperate to Get into Television. Don't get me wrong, I quite like radio people really, they're sort of, well, homely really aren't they?...no, let's not beat about the bush, they're ugly. Just walk along the *Loose Ends* corridor at Broadcasting House. Sorry, you'd think you were either in some sort of Hieronymus Bosch painting, or visiting an amputee ward. But go along to Television Centre, people are glamorous. They spend more money on their Grecian 2000 than is spent on the entire yearly budget for *You and Yours*. TV people go to all the hip joints — radio people have plastic ones fitted. TV people don't wear cardigans or airtex underpants like radio people. And they have the full complement of limbs. They're beautiful people, I'm beautiful people. I've got Anthony Howard's bone structure, and frankly I make Jonathan Ross look like Magnus Pyke.

FX **MATTRESS BEING RHYTHMICALLY BOUNCED UPON, SPRINGS BOIIINGING.**

VLS Shut up! Will you please shut up down there!

FX **BOUNCING CONTINUES. WHIPPING AND WHOOPING SOUNDS.**

VLS It's Saturday evening in my luxurious penthouse flat in York. Downstairs my concierge, Mrs Tribly, is practising mixed trampolining with a seascout friend she sometimes locks in for days on end.

FX **PHONE RINGS.**

VLS Oh no, that's the phone. I'd better take the call in the relative quietness of my wardrobe.

FX **LIFTS RECEIVER.**

VLS Hello, speaking from the relative quietness of my wardrobe. Ah, hello Mr Gardhouse... It's Mr Gardhouse who, having seen my recent Bob Says Opportunity Knocks appearance disguised as eight-year-old songbird Toni Warne, knows I yearn and am destined for TV stardom. Frankly, he grovels to keep me on his rather sad little programme.

FX **MR GARDHOUSE'S VOICE THROUGH EARPIECE.**

VLS No...sorry Gardhouse, you've had your chance... it's too late...Don't try threats, I've seen Margaret Howard's so-called heavies, and they'd never get their Zimmer frames up my staircase...Oh I see, that's *very* nice, I can have Ned's job can I?...that's very loyal, how can you be so callous?...he's given you the best years of his life... Oh yes, and how will he pay for the electrolysis sessions and all that prosthetic equipment he has to use?...I'm sorry, I have got bigger fish to fry.

FX   SLAMS RECEIVER DOWN. CUT TO DEEP FAT FRYING.

VLS   It's pathetic really. Without me, Gardhouse will end up as Producer of the Long Range Shipping Forecast. Still, *plus ça change,* as my old Granny used to say, *dans la nuit tous les chats sont gris, chacun à son goût et* 'ow you zay *où sont les neiges d'antan,* unfortunately she rambled a bit towards the end.

FX   ROMANTIC PIANO MUSIC.

VLS   A box of Black Magic, and a romantic TV dinner for two. Tonight, it's Spicy Eggs Indienne though, to be honest, I do prefer them out of de hen.

FX   COCK CROWING, PIANO CONTINUES.

VLS   A litre bottle of Seven Up, which reminds me, I really must clip my goat's nails, they're beginning to ladder the Draylon suite, a tube of delay cream...

FX   GOAT BLEATS.

VLS   ...and as Goatie gently nibbles at my earlobe, it's off with the Ronnie Aldrich.

FX   'I SAY SID' 'WHAT EDDIE?' 'BUM-BUMS, WEE-WEES, GOING TO THE TOILET AND DARKIES. EH SID' 'YEAH?' 'SID' 'YEAH?' 'SID' YEAH?' 'SID' 'YEAH?' 'SID, WHAT'D THEE 'AD FOR THEE DINNER?' 'WELL EDDIE, I 'AD EGGS INDIENNE' 'I PREFER 'EM OUT OF DE 'EN MESELF SID' ALL TV SOUND QUALITY.

VLS   Ooo, they're good

FX   'OO, YOU'RE A PICKLE, YES YOU ARE, A PICKLE'. SWITCHES OFF.

VLS   Ooo, they're good they are. But, to be fair, they're crap aren't they? Imagine stooping to gags of that calibre. I can do better, I want my own TV show, and I want it now. If only the nice Mr Grade from BBC1 would telephone me at the end of this...

FX   4″ PAUSE. PHONE RINGS.

VLS   sentence.

FX   ANSWERS PHONE. 'O'GRADY SAYS DO THIS'.

VLS   (*obsequiously*) Oh, Mr Grade, Oh may I say what an honour this is, of course I'm merely the lowest speck of pond filth, you're too good for this earth, God bless yer heart, braces, oh braces...

VLS   (*close mike over phone call*) A warning to anybody trying to get into television. Don't overdo the smarm. I became so very unctuous and greasy that, before he could offer me a job, I suffered a serious attack of spontaneous oleagination,

FX   BUBBLING SOUNDS, BURBLING.

VLS   rapidly turning into a pool of slime.

FX   RAIN. VOICE OVER TANNOY 'THERE WILL BE NO PLAY TODAY AT WIMBLEDON, NO PLAY TODAY AT WIMBLEDON.'

VLS   Before I knew what was happening, I'd completely liquified and Mrs Tribly, mistaking me for a pool of goat sick, hosed me down the drain, a disposition hardly befitting a rising star in the televisual firmament. Luckily, by the natural and mysterious processes of the rain cycle, I found myself next day pelting down on the Centre Court at Wimbledon. No play on Monday? That was me.

FX   CUT TO FLAT, WHIPPET WHINING, RICHARD CLAYDERMAN ON PIANO.

VLS   It's Tuesday evening. Back at the flat, Mrs Tribly offers no apology or solace. She's just landed a plum job as Chief Airport Virginity Tester at Leeds/Bradford, and is practising on the whippet. I ask her to leave, but she insists on administering a strong purgative to me.

FX   UNPLEASANT INTESTINAL ERUPTION. ANGUISHED SCREAM.

VLS   I have an out-of-body experience and, after she's gone, I telephone the local Job Line for some ideas on how to be a TV star.

FX   SILENCE.

VLS   Unfortunately, at this point, there should have been the sound effect of a ringing tone, but I made the mistake this morning of buying frozen sound effects and they don't seem to have thawed properly yet. Bear with me while I just pop them into the microwave.

FX   MICROWAVE DOOR SHUT. SWITCHED ON.

VLS I think that's nearly ready.
FX MICROWAVE DING.
VLS Right, now for the Job Line.
FX PHONE RINGS. TAPED VOICE, GENTLE MUSIC BEHIND IT. 'WELCOME TO THE ALL-COMPUTERISED WIGGINGTON JOB CENTRE HELPLINE. PLEASE STATE NOW WHICH CATEGORY YOU REQUIRE AND YOU WILL BE CONNECTED TO OUR TAPE SERVICE.'
VLS Well, I want to be a star really.
FX VOICE: 'THANKYOU. THE FOLLOWING OPPORTUNITIES ARE CURRENTLY AVAILABLE IN TELEVISION, FOR THOSE WHO WISH TO BE TV STARS. ALL APPLICANTS MUST HAVE ONE OF THE FOLLOWING GRADES: LEW OR MICHAEL GRADE IN THE FAMILY IS PREFERRED, ALTHOUGH IN SOME CASES, CANDIDATES WITH AN EQUIVALENT DELFONT OR FOX MAY ALSO BE CONSIDERED. UNFORTUNATELY, WENHAMS ARE NO LONGER A RECOGNISED QUALIFICATION. ALL TELEVISION APPLICANTS MUST HAVE 'O' LEVELS IN BACK-STABBING, AND AT LEAST A CSE IN SAYING "THAT WAS WONDERFUL DARLINGS" TO ARTISTES, AND WHEN SAID ARTISTES HAVE LEFT THE STUDIO, SAYING LOUDLY TO EVERYONE THAT THAT PERSON IS SACKED, AND LAUGHING. NEEDLESS TO SAY, UGLY PEOPLE NEED NOT APPLY. INSTEAD, TRY EITHER LOCAL GOVERNMENT OR RADIO 4. HERE IS A LIST OF TELEVISION VACANCIES: BBC TELEVISION'S *PLAYSCHOOL* REQUIRES A RESIDENT ONE-FINGERED VENEREOLOGIST. MUST HAVE OWN RUBBER GLOVE AND BE ABLE TO PLAY TAMBOURINE AND PRETEND TO ENJOY THEMSELVES.'
VLS No, that's not for me.
FX THE METEOROLOGICAL OFFICE REQUIRE A STUNT MAN FOR IAN MACGASKILL, AND A BLIND SEAMSTRESS AS A TAILOR FOR MICHAEL FISH.
VLS No, I don't think so
FX THERE IS ALSO A VACANCY FOR NIGHT WORK ON BBC2. THE NETWORK REQUIRES A PERSON TO BE THE LITTLE WHITE DOT ON THE SCREEN AFTER CLOSEDOWN. APPLICANTS MUST BE COMPLETELY SPHERICAL, AND ABLE TO STAND IN A PITCH-BLACK FIELD, WEAR A WHITE SUIT, AND RUN AWAY FROM THE CAMERA WHILE GOING 'BOOOOOOOOOOOOOOOO'.
FX CUT TO SILENCE.
VLS Fortunately, there was at least one job for which I was perfectly suited. Up at the crack of noon, I was at Television Centre being screen-tested for my prime-time TV slot.
FX CAMP VOICE: 'OK VICTOR DARLING, JUMP ON TO THE DANSETTE NOW PLEASE, THAT'S SUPER.'
VLS It's degrading, but what you can hear is my debut as the BBC1 revolving globe. Owing to my peculiar physiognomy, Mr Grade considered me ideal for the role. It's a head job. I stand in a black cloak on the turntable of an old Dansette, revolving at thirty-three-and-a-third.
FX 'SLOW DOWN WHEN YOU GET TO BRITAIN, DON'T FLAP YOUR EARS, WE'LL GO FOR A TAKE...RIGHT, RUN IT DARLING, AND CUE THE MUSIC NOW.' NATIONAL ANTHEM STARTS.
VLS I wear thick blue and green make-up. Look closely, my nose is Southern India, my chin the Republic of Zaire, my left earlobe Guatemala, and my shaving rash the Philippines. Unfortunately an allergy struck last week and fifteen million people saw a live reenactment of Krakatoa East of Java erupting from my right nostril. Still, it's a living, or rather it's not, because they gave me the push when I yawned last week and parted the Red Sea. Never mind, I suppose I'll have to slum it back in steam radio with you load of goat's phlegm in the studio. Can I have my money now please?

BBC SOUND EFFECTS INDEX

Spittoon
See also Sputum

Spittoon

Single gouts entering empty spittoon. (From 78 disc) – 1942 – 38″		
Multiple gouts entering nearly full spittoon. (Recorded at World Convention of Spittoon Users, with cheering from small crowd. Kentucky) – Nov 82 – 2′14″	EC197B(s)	b05

Spleen — EC48A — f03

Spleen being vented (Plymouth) – Aug 76 – 32″	EC4G2	b03
Unvented spleen (Plymouth) – Aug 76 – 2′08″	EC4G2	b04

Split Infinitive
To being rent asunder from its infinitive – May 54 – 06″ — EC196A(s) — f02

Spondee
One-legged poet reciting two long syllables. (From 78 disc) Jan 75 –8″ — EC1106H — f13

Squid

Distress call of injured squid – Sep 57 – 1′56″	NH113Z	b03
Sick squid being handed to Tom O'Connor as payment of his £6 commission for use of very old joke – Aug 87 – 15″	EC103A	b02

Stableboy

Stableboy saddling stallion (Ascot) – Dec 76 – 1′02″	EC184B	b07
Stableboy mounting filly, police siren, handcuffs snapping shut, shouts of 'disgusting' – Dec 76 – 2′45″	EC184B	b08

Stage-struck
Old thespian being struck by stage – Nov 75 – 01″ — EC19D (s) — b01

Stage whisper
Old thespian whispering to another (Old Vic, 117 decibels) – May 61 – 47″ — EC82B — f09

Staple
African Bushmen enjoying meal of small bent pieces of metal, paying Tom O'Connor £6 commission for supplying their staple diet (Kalahari, from 78 disc) – Feb 38 –2′07″ — EC500X — f02

Steatopygia
Steatopygic radio talk-show hostess sitting down – May 86 – 08″ — EC1106H — b11

SHERINE/GRADESKY INTERNATIONAL ARTISTE CONGLOMERATES inc IN ASSOCIATION WITH LA DELFONT SOUTH OCKENDON CREMATORIUM PLAYERS:

THE *LOOSE ENDS* ALL-STAR CHRISTMAS PANTO ON ICE

★★

PETER PAN

STARRING

POL ('THE KILLING FIELD') POT AS TINKERBELL
'OOOer mother ... I've lost me droowars'

WITH

PRESIDENT ('MINE'S A PINT') ZIA OF PAKISTAN
AS MRS DARLING '30 miles from London
and still no sign of Dick'

RONNIE ('I AM DEAD') RENALDE
AS A DEAD PERSON ON STAGE (' — ')

ANITA ('WHO?') HARRIS AS SOMEONE WHO SLAPS
HER THIGHS 'Eradicate the Kulaks as a social class!'

EMPEROR ('TV'S MR 'ELLO 'ELLO') BOKASSA
AS WIDOW TWANKY
'More salt with me boiled baby nancy'

70

AND VARIETY FEATS OF DERRING-DO FROM—

BRIAN ('ALL IS FLUX')
HERACLITUS, who will
amaze both young and old
as he steps into the
same river TWICE!
(without safety net)

NOEL ('COME ON DOWN') EDMONDS.
T H R I L L with delight as he demonstrates his
rare ability to shine a torch in his left ear
and allows it to pass unimpeded straight
out through the right ear undimmed. Not to be missed!

FREDDIE (FUCK) STARR who will remind the audience
of black and white television, and come on stage and
say fuck a lot and shout at the band and then bite the
head off a hamster.

★★★★ PLUS PLUS PLUS PLUS PLUS PLUS TELEVISION'S 'YOU'RE A STAR' SPOT.

EVERY NIGHT,
FRESH FROM THE M62,
WE WILL BRING YOU THE
MOST RECENT CRITICAL ROAD VICTIM
— IN SHOCK — WHO WILL BE ASKED
TO SING REQUESTS FROM THE
AUDIENCE. (We guarantee
no hospital registered 'stable',
'very poorly', 'comfortable'
or 'out of danger' cases. Accompanied by
members of the St. John's Ambulance Brigade).

AND ...

HARRY ('DOES ANYONE SMELL
FORMALDEHYDE?') WORTH —
who will do the same bloody
routine with a shop window
and bore the arse off everyone
in the Green Room after by
talking about how close he is
to Lew Grade, which turns out
to be not very close at all after
Lew Grade turns up in the
Green Room and says
'Harry WHO?'

Christmas in NWI

Scene: *The North London home of Simon and Joanna Stringalong.*
Simon is on the telephone. Joanna is on the gin.
Neither is happy.

SIMON She must be out.

JOANNA A schoolteacher? Why isn't she at home marking books? Let it ring.

SIMON Oh *hello*. Is that Miss Henstridge? This is Simon, Jessica Stringalong's father. I'm sorry if I'm ringing at an impossibly late hour.

JOANNA It's only half past eight!

SIMON ... I just hope I'm not interrupting a candlelit *diner à deux*. But what I'm ringing about, Miss Henstridge... Pru *(to Joanna)* she says I've to call her Pru...

JOANNA Pru!

SIMON What I'm ringing about, Pru, is that we've just put little Jessica to bed in what quite honestly was a very distressed condition. The thing was she came home from school with this letter...

JOANNA Letter!

SIMON ... about the Nativity play. All pretty straightforward. Probably wouldn't have even read it...

JOANNA You wouldn't. You never do.

SIMON ... only Joanna, my wife, gave it to me so I idly glanced through it to see what part Jessica was playing only I couldn't find her. I couldn't find her *at all*, until I came right to the very end, the bottom of the bill, as it were, where it says 'Pauline Greenwood, Kevin Strutt, and Jessica Stringalong... *icicles*'. Now Joanna, my wife, and I may be getting hold of the wrong end of the stick, Pru, and it may be these icicles

have a crucial part to play...

JOANNA *(snatching the phone)* ... but just judging from the billing it doesn't look like it. What the hell do these icicles do, Pru?

Simon snatches the phone back

SIMON Sorry. That was my wife. The icicles do what, Pru? They drip. I see. *(To Joanna)* They drip.

JOANNA Let me. The point is, Pru, do they drip verbally? No. I thought so. She's just an extra — A walk-on! Jessica! I was in the Marlowe Society!

SIMON What is worrying Mrs Stringalong and myself, Pru, is that in last year's show Jessica had quite an interesting little part as...

JOANNA A Bethlehem housewife.

SIMON A Bethlehem housewife.

JOANNA Give it here. We hear a great deal about falling educational standards and as you probably know, Pru, my husband and I only decided to put Jessica into the state system after a great deal of heartsearching and now we find that last year she played a housewife and this year she just drips, what kind of progress is that? Last year Jessica had a long speech. *Tell her...*

SIMON Last year Jessica had a speech, now what was it...

JOANNA 'You can't move in the middle of Bethlehem. I understand there's not a bed to be had.'

SIMON   'You can't move in the middle of
         Bethlehem. I understand there's not a
         bed to be had.' And there was a bit
         more (and I'm not sure this didn't
         come off the top of Jessica's little
         head).

JOANNA   'Next thing you know they'll be
         sleeping in the stables.'

SIMON   That was about the gist of it. 'You
         can't move in the middle of
         Bethlehem. I understand there's not a
         bed to be had. Next thing you know
         they'll be sleeping in the stables.' Quite
         an interesting part with a significant
         piece of plot-laying. Which Jessica did
         quite superbly.

JOANNA   Peggy Ashcroft.

SIMON   Very clear. Very sharp. 'You can't
         move in the middle of Bethlehem. I
         understand there's not a bed to be
         had. Next thing you know they'll be
         sleeping in the stables.' And this year
         she just drips. It's very disappointing.

JOANNA   It's bloody scandalous.

SIMON   We, who so much enjoyed her
         performance last Christmas, were
         looking forward to this Yuletide to see
         what she made of a more taxing role.
         I'm sure she'll make a good icicle... a
         superb icicle... and knowing Jessica
         she'll throw herself heart and soul into
         the part.

JOANNA   But why the hell isn't there more of a
         part for her to throw herself heart and
         soul into, Pru?

SIMON   My wife, again, I'm afraid. She is a bit
         upset, yes. I imagine from the cast list
         that you're filling out the gospel story a
         little. Icicles hanging by the wall, Dick
         the Shepherd blowing his nail and so
         on.

JOANNA   What about Dick the Shepherd, who's
         got that?

SIMON   What about Dick the Shepherd, Pru?
         She'd probably do that rather well.
         There is a distinction between sucking
         her thumb and blowing her nail but
         only a purist would know the
         difference. Dick's gone? Pity. Now who
         else is there in the gospel story?

JOANNA   *(seizing the phone again)* Who the hell's
         playing Mary?
         Sorry. Who is playing Mary as a
         matter of interest? Oh. Tracy
         Broadbent. Tracy Broadbent? Jesus
         Christ!

SIMON   Yes, we do know Tracy as a matter of
         fact. Her mother used to clean for us.
         Yes. Tracy was Herod last year. I
         remember. And she is not good, Pru.
         And as Herod she was way over the
         top. I couldn't believe in her, frankly.
         Tracy's Herod just didn't work for
         either of us. You also have to
         remember, Pru, that Tracy comes from
         a one parent family and that one
         parent, her mother, goes out to work
         so looked at purely from a Box Office
         point of view Tracy Broadbent won't
         bring anybody in at all. You aren't
         going to get a line round the block
         with little Tracy. Whereas with Jessica
         in the role you sell half a dozen tickets
         on her name alone. There's us. Her
         granny. Her granny's friend, Mrs
         Beavers. Ulla, our au pair. Ignaz,
         Ulla's Turkish boyfriend. I mean it's
         House Full notices practically before
         you open the Box Office.

JOANNA   Tracy Broadbent bit Jessica.

SIMON   Joanna has just reminded me that
         Tracy bit little Jessica. That's hardly
         my idea of the Virgin Mary. She didn't

go around biting people, so far as we know. Well I agree, Pru. Tracy probably is disturbed but do you want a disturbed child in the role of the Blessed Mother? I see. Mary is being played as a battered wife. And baby Jesus a battered baby. So what does that make Joseph? Gay? I was a fool to ask. *(To Joanna)* Gay.

JOANNA   Is Joseph cast?

SIMON   Is he cast? Jessica can play gay, I'm sure. And she wouldn't object to appearing in travesty. He's going to be black.

JOANNA   Well she could black up.

SIMON   You don't seem to understand, Pru. This is an adaptable little girl.

JOANNA   What about the Three Wise Men?

SIMON   Yes. What about the Three Wise Men? There are no Three Wise Men? Not as such. So what are they? Three Social Workers of Camden. I see. So as I understand it, Pru, the story line is this: Herod is the Chancellor of the Exchequer making swingeing cuts in the social services, putting battered Baby Jesus at risk and he is rescued by the Three Social Workers of Camden. It's uncanny how it all fits in. The potency of myth, I suppose.
But no part for little Jessica. Let's get back to this icicle, the part for which you've got her pencilled in, where is it hanging from? I see. The bloated body of capitalism.

JOANNA   *(shaking her head vigorously)* No, no, no. Sorry. Forget it.

SIMON   I'm not sure that we are wholly in agreement with that, Pru. Mrs Stringalong's father is quite prominent in wholesale floor coverings and I think we would feel that if little Jessica was going to be involved in making a direct political statement such as that, we might well have to keep her at home. No, Pru. We are not just talking about a Nativity play. We are talking about the most precious thing in the world, a child's mind. I'm sorry.
No, I'm sorry. That is final. *(Pause)* Pickets? What sort of Pickets? *(To Joanna)* There's a part as a picket.

JOANNA   Are they speaking pickets?

SIMON   Speaking pickets and flying pickets. Like flying ballet, you mean. That sounds wonderful!

JOANNA   What's the scene?

SIMON   A hotel in Bethlehem. Trust House. Yes, yes. Go on. Catering staff on strike, yes, yes? I get the picture. An enraged guest, played by Rhoda Allnatt, comes out of the hotel and says 'What's happened to Peace on Earth, Goodwill to all men?' And Jessica shouts out 'Scab!' That sounds marvellous.

JOANNA   Does she get billing?

SIMON   Would she get billing at all? I don't think we'd want anything special. 'And Jessica Stringalong as The Picket' would be ideal.
I don't think you'll regret it, Pru. I mean all those exciting things happening and Jessica just stood there, dripping her little heart out. No. 'Scab!' is better. And if I know Jessica she'll really throw herself into it. I'll see she gets down to learning her word at the earliest opportunity. Goodbye and Merry Christmas.

BY PAUL BURBRIDGE

As AN INTEMPERATE and passionate listener to the wireless I was very surprised to hear that certain persons have been pestering the good officers of the British Broadcasting Corporation and demanding to be allowed to be heard on that oldest of sound arenas *Any Fascists* — oh, I do beg your pardon — *Any Questions*, the light in here isn't very good. Do you know the whole story?

There is a frightful programme on the Home Service called *ThrowUp* or *Feedback* or *HowlRound* or some such drivel. It's one of those monstrous ideas that can only emerge from the dripping caverns of the mind of the criminally insane or the Oxford educated. It seems to exist entirely for those unconscionable members of our society who demand that the wireless should be some kind of genteel hermitage upon which the language, idiom and vitality of the real world never impinges. These poor afflicted creatures spend their time with an ear against the speaker counting occurrences of the word 'bugger'. If I had a large amount of money I should certainly found a hospital for those whose grip upon the world is so tenuous that they can be severely offended by words and phrases and yet remain all

DR TREFUSIS'S ANNUAL LECTURE TO THE WALTHAMSTOW COLLEGE OF KNOWLEDGE

Whither the Home Service?

Précised by his amanuensis Stephen Fry

unoffended by the injustice, violence and oppression that howls daily about our ears. The only advice I would give anyone who loves the wireless is to write in each time you hear a drama or a comedy that compromises on language. How can I listen to a play that is supposed to be a reflection of real life where characters say nothing but 'bother' and 'dash' all the time? It is a grotesque offence to the integrity of art. Unless you are heard the gibbering lunatics will carry the day. However, this is really by the way.

Feedback is a Radio 4 programme and therefore is naturally a kind of sanctuary for the mentally deficient — you mustn't think I'm biting the hand that feeds me here, I happen to know that the small but charming audience for my little wireless essays is composed of none but the judicious and the wise. I am aware that none of you has ever written in to complain at the phrase 'bloody bastard', you're not insane. Most of the *Feedback* audience, however, *is* insane. Quite appallingly potty. Barking mad to a man. Imagine, then, the length, breadth, depth and height of my dismay on hearing that from amongst this audience was to be culled a pool or well or reservoir of potential guests on *Any Fascists —* **Questions**, really the light is *appalling*. Two hundred of the ripest bedlamites in Britain have written in to be considered as the Ordinary Person On the Panel.

We have to thank for this barbarous notion a deluded soul, a forlorn stumbler in the darkness of unreason who wrote to *Feedback* complaining that the politicians, authors and financial rapists who usually comprise the bench are not representative of the wide world. 'Let us hear the voice of the common man' is the cry. How you could get more common than Peter Marsh, Gerald Kauffman or Edwina Currie or other such ghastly confections I should be very interested to know. However, the motion has been carried and certain persons will soon be heard on the programme.

Any FashQuestions is one of those institutions designed to provoke anger and precipitate apoplexy across the kingdom. If you see a purple-faced person shouting and screaming at a wireless set then there is a better than ever chance that it is *Any Questions* that is exercising them. It is astonishing how articulate one can become when alone and raving at a radio. Arguments and counter-arguments, rhetoric and bombast flow from one's lips like scurf from the hair of a bank manager. But the BBC in its wisdom provides a remedy. *Any Answers.* It is precisely there to prove how much more worthless, even than a politician's views, are the opinions of the wireless listening public. That is where to go if you wish to embarrass the intelligent members of your family by discussing concepts you barely understand, like law and order and morality. It is to *Any Answers* that you turn when you want to deliver yourself of your prejudices and hatreds. *Any Answers* will be an important document for future generations, when they seek to examine the decline in literacy, courtesy and understanding that finally propelled the twentieth century into an abyss of selfish individualism and unneighbourly aggression. But *Any Questions* has a more immediate funciton.

We live, my dears, don't we, in a democracy of sorts. A democracy is a means whereby we channel our contempt for our fellow man into a lively scorn for those elected to represent him. Kindly men and women accept invitations to appear on *Any Questions* to absorb the hatred that would otherwise spill on to the streets. We know who these people are, we pay them handsomely for their sacrifice. They come to stand for the intemperate views that are killing our country. If we dare to replace these souls with ordinary people I fear for what may happen. I know that if I were driving my Wolseley around Cambridge and I happened to hear some lawyer or housewife talking about moral fabric or the family unit I should very likely swerve on to the pavement and massacre a dozen family units there and then.

No, no, it's too dangerous. Let the maniacs continue to write their letters and let the public men do the speaking. I must hand you back to London now and leave you with this public maniac. Nedwin.

THE *LOOSE ENDS* 'BEING THERE' KIT PART TWO

BE A GUEST ON *LOOSE ENDS*

SIMPLY STICK A PASSPORT PHOTOGRAPH OF YOURSELF ONTO THE MARKED SECTION, AND ACTUALLY BE A GUEST MAKING A FUNNY AND POPULAR JOKE.

PART V

in which Harold Coaltart, BBC Commissionaire, poses the ontological question, 'Will the last word ever spoken be why, why, why...?'*

Do you know something? When the chips are down in downtown Warley, I always say to myself, Harold, I say, the chips are down. I'm like that. I'm sorry, I'm a bit of a thinker. I did start an Open University course ... well, I say start, I sent off for the brochure, but it seemed to be written in a foreign language, so I did night classes in Ford Cortina maintenance instead. I think I made the right decision ... logical positivism is one thing, but getting a regular 30 miles to the gallon IN TRAFFIC is quite another. Still, won't beat about the bush, Harold Coaltart was up against it and Mr Sippi certainly wasn't coming up with any suggestions as regards escaping the impending inferno. The Hammond organ was playing the closing bars of 'Roses of Picardie', the bit that goes 'it's the rose that I keep in my heart', and I said to myself, Harold, the chips are down. Then I said to myself, Harold, you've already said that, and quite frankly it's time for action. Because as I always say, when the going gets tough, the tough get going. I have to say by the way that in the confines of a casket, as our American brethren refer to it, Mr Sippi's personal freshness left quite a lot to be desired, and I don't think I'm speaking out of turn if I remark that, had I had an aerosol deodorant with me, he, without beating about the bush, would have been the first to benefit from its use, although at such extreme temperatures as we were expecting, said deodorant would have been liable to explode and you don't want none of that nonsense in the enclosed confines of a coffin, thank you very much.

Well, on the digital watch that I got with 50 gallons of 4 star, I noticed that the temperature setting had reached 3,000 degrees Centigrade. I like it warm, but not too warm, which is why we go to Canvey Island every year and not Benidorm like some of the pond filth living on the estate. Anyway, I was just about to undo my collar button when suddenly the burners switched off and the atmosphere became a little less close. Acting on impulse alone, I suddenly broke into my rendition of 'Chirpy Chirpy Cheep Cheep', a popular song of the 1970s by a group whose name for the moment escapes me, however the words went: 'Last night I saw your mamma walking alone ... oooo eeee chirpy chirpy cheep cheep.' Imagine my surprise when I was told later that several members of the congregation had passed out with shock and that the pathetically optimistic Mrs Sippi took to a chainsaw and sliced open the top of the coffin only to find her husband still as deceased as ever, and me halfway through the second chorus. It turned out that somebody at the crematorium had forgotten to put two bob in the gas, which was okay for me, but a half-finished job for Mr Sippi. Of course it was left to me, Muggins here, to fork out the loose change to carbonise said neighbour, so all's well that ends well, and it was off, some of us in ambulances, chez Sippi for refreshments.

Nice spread at the Sippi household. Ham and pickle, fish paste, cheese and tomato, celery, salad cream, some nice Battenburg, mince pies, some wine and some rock cakes, the single donation from Brenda and myself, which for some reason were so good that everyone agreed they were too good to be eaten. Flushed with too many glasses of sherry, Mr Lobley from No. 16 jumped up on to the table and sang his version of the Tom Jones hit, 'The Green Green Grass of Home'. Unfortunately this all became rather unsavoury when Mr Lobley forgot where he was and, in an almost possessed, trance-like state, imitated the Welshman's lewd pelvic thrusts, rendering Mrs Sippi unconscious for the twelfth time that afternoon. An amusing thought suddenly struck me. Mrs Sippi's name

was very similar to that of a North American river. Chuckling heartily to myself, I mentioned this to her, but she seemed to have let grief dampen her sense of humour.

Then Brenda had a bright idea and suggested it was about time to share out Mr Sippi's personal effects, though Mrs Sippi, in her crazed state, insisted that her husband's dying wish was that she should be the sole beneficiary. How we laughed, as I emptied out the drawers of the sideboard. I won't beat about the bush, finding nothing of value there, I was up the stairs like a whippet, and into his bedroom wardrobe, where I discovered a large old tin once containing crisps on which was writ large the legend: DO NOT OPEN OR ELSE N.N. SIPPI. How dare you, I thought, HOW DARE YOU? I'm not being ordered about by a dead person with no rights ... who does he think he is, I thought, and quick as a flash I whipped off the lid ... only to discover a huge 17-foot tarantula spider, highly poisonous and with great hairy legs, just about to go for my throat.

Will Harold Coaltart be savaged by the giant spider? Turn to p.100 to find out.

SHERINE ENTERPRISES OFFER YOU THE CHANCE TO OWN A REPLICA OF JONATHAN ROSS'S DREAM MACHINE.

HUMILIATE WORKING-CLASS AND VULGAR CAPRI DRIVERS WHO HAVE MOCK VELVET STEERING WHEEL COVERS, SUITS HANGING UP IN THE BACK, DOGS WITH NODDING HEADS AND FLUFFY DICE HANGING IN THE WINDOW

1) 'INVERSION IS THE ESSENCE OF COMEDY' SAYS MARTIN FISHER, HEAD OF LIGHT ENTERTAINMENT RADIO.

2) THIS SATIRISES THE MOST COMMON NAMES FOUND ON COUNCIL ESTATES IN THE SOUTH EAST.

SANDRA & CLINT

THE FLUFFY DICE MOBILE MAKES THE POINT!

4) THIS IS AN ARROW.

3) THIS IS NOT A CAR. IT IS A FLUFFY DICE, (cf 1 : 'Inversion')

5) THIS IS A ROGUE BOGEY WHICH HAS BEEN LEFT BY A MEMBER OF YOUR FAMILY AND PRESSED-DRIED INTO THE BOOK. THE DILEMMA YOU'RE LEFT WITH IS, DO YOU PICK IT OFF, WHICH IS PRETTY NASTY ANYWAY, AND YOU MAY TEAR THE BOOK, OR DO YOU LEAVE IT THERE AS A CONFESSION OF THE DISGUSTING HABITS OF SOME MEMBER OF YOUR KITH OR POSSIBLY KIN, WHO PROBABLY IS THE SORT OF PERSON WHO DRIVES A FORD CAPRI IN THE FIRST PLACE AND DOESN'T UNDERSTAND JACK SHIT ABOUT THE THALIAN MUSE AND THINKS THIS BOOK IS SOME SORT OF OVER MONOGRAMMED HANKY THE SORT OF PERSON I HAD IN MY FAMILY ACTUALLY, YOU KNOW THEY'RE ALWAYS PUTTING THEIR HEAD ROUND THE BEDROOM DOOR WITHOUT KNOCKING WHEN YOU'RE JUST ABOUT TO HAVE A GOOD OLD FASHIONED SESSION OF TWANGING THE WIRE AND HE ALWAYS GOT HOLD OF THE REMOTE CONTROL ON THE TELLY AND HE KEPT ZAPPING AROUND THE CHANNELS WHEN I WAS TRYING TO WATCH NEIGHBOURS AND HE ALWAYS NICKED MY PURPLE SOCKS AND THEY'RE MINE I BOUGHT THEM LAST MONTH AT TOP MAN THEY'RE NOT YOURS AND KEEP YOUR BLOODY THIEVING HANDS OFF MY MAGAZINES THEY WERE STUCK TOGETHER LAST TIME I LOOKED MUM!! ... MUM!!! ... MUM!!!! WILL YOU TELL DAVID NOT TO NICK MY AFTERSHAVE IT'S .... I'm sorry. I have not been very well recently.
Yes. I am
taking medication.

HER GREAT GRANDFATHER CHANGED THE FACE OF THE
TWENTIETH CENTURY WITH HIS STARTLING INSIGHT
INTO HUMAN PSYCHOLOGY — NOW LET HIS GREAT
GRAND-DAUGHTER HELP YOU...

Emma's Problem Page

Dear Emma
I think you are really beautiful, I watch you on telly
and think you're completely fantastic and on the
radio you're the best thing ever.
  signed
Lots and lots of people

EMMA'S REPLY: Thank you very much.

Dear Emma
Why is everyone on *Loose Ends* so self-indulgent?
  signed
The duty Office

EMMA'S REPLY: A Fish

Dear Emma
I would really like to present on *Loose Ends*. I am a
first class journalist but my parents aren't famous, I
don't have a regional accent and have never owned a
Filofax. Do I stand a chance?
  signed
B. Hanrohan

EMMA'S REPLY: No.

Dear Emma
I really hate *Loose Ends*.
  signed
J Archer, Cambs.

EMMA'S REPLY: Good.

Dear Emma
How much do you know about psychology?
  signed
M Howard, Dulwich

EMMA'S REPLY: Lots thanks.

Loose Ends and its audience

THE D.G.   KICKS ASS

FX   *MARY POPPINS* SOUNDTRACK.
      'SUPERCALLIFRAGELISTICEXPIALIDOCI-
      OUS.'
VLS   It's Saturday evening and, being a *Loose Ends*
      megastar, I'm at the cinema in cognito. Cognito
      is a beautiful little Italian island, but frankly it's a
      sod of a distance to go just to see *Mary Poppins*.
      Worse still, they've dubbed the soundtrack into
      Neapolitan dialect and ruined Mr Van Dyke's
      authentic rendition of the Cockney accent.
FX   HALF-COCKNEY, HALF-NEAPOLITAN
      VOICE 'IN SULLE VECCHIE MELÉ E
      PERÉ. COR BLIMEY MATE.' CUT TO
      JUMBO JET INTERIOR. CANNED MUSIC.
VLS   Flying back, I drown my sorrows on a heady mix
      of brown ale and Cherry B. Mrs Tribly is not on
      the plane because, while in the cinema, she gets

the hots for the Italian projectionist, and is now in fatuated with him. Fatuated is a small town in Communicado. The Air Hostess comforts me and slips me a 12-pack of Duty-Free canned laughter.

FX   'OH, THANK YOU MISS,' RING-PULL, HISS, SHORT BURST OF CANNED LAUGHTER.

VLS   I arrive back at my luxury penthouse flat in York. My whippet is looking a little under the weather, its bowels removed, liver ripped out, kidney and spleen plonked on the mantelpiece and its brain sucked out through its ears. To quote Edgar Lustgarten 'Pshaw! Someone's been up to no good, I'll be bound.' I find its gonads in the butterdish with a note written in dog-blood attached. It says 'Stop this persecution of Thora Hird on *Loose Ends*, or Mrs Tribly is next. We play it rough at the C of E. Sincerely, a well-wisher.'

FX   LIQUIDISER.

VLS   Oh well, waste not want not, as my old granny used to say. I hoover up the bits and plop them in the blender. Good 'n' thick, and I throw in the lead, 'cos it's high in fibre. *Et voilà,* a cheap and nourishing Fictional Whippet Purée. I sip it through a straw, while musing on the curious relationship between Radio 4 and its audience. Let me explain, in symbiotic terms:

FX   MUSIC *THE BODY IN QUESTION.*

VLS   *Loose Ends* has an audience of two million. Research tells us that the vast majority, and that includes you, live in the Home Counties and are from Social Group Bl. You listening now are young marrieds, probably called Simeon or Natasha, and you call each other darling, and you warm up your croissants in the Aga, don't you? And Natasha wears Laura Ashley frocks, and buys recycled organic tampons, and you have hideous children called Dominic and Tristram, you buy Perrier at Sainsbury's, and have wooden lavatory seats. In short, if you listen to this programme, and read this book, you are revoltingly middle-class, and anyway you're probably not listening to this programme because to you Radio 4 is merely aural wallpaper.

To prove that you don't listen to my ratings-saving masterpieces, I will suck on my microphone, inhale the sound of your living-room, and blow it out for everyone to hear.

FX   INHALE, EXHALE NOISILY. SOUNDS OF

HER GREAT GRANDFATHER CHANGED THE FACE OF THE TWENTIETH CENTURY BY BEING A REALLY GOOD DOCTOR — NOW LET HIS GREAT GRAND-DAUGHTER SORT OUT YOUR MOST EMBARRASSING PERSONAL QUERIES...

Dear Doctor Emma

Dear Doctor Emma
I think you are really beautiful, I watch you on telly and think you're completely fantastic and on the radio you're the best thing ever. Is this a problem?
  signed
Worried, Liverpool

DOCTOR EMMA'S REPLY: No.

Dear Doctor Emma
I have a nasty red spotty rash under one of my arms. What should I do?
  signed
Concerned, Manchester

DOCTOR EMMA'S REPLY: Put Savlon on it and if that doesn't work, scratch it.

Dear Doctor Emma
Are you a real doctor?
  signed
M Howard, Dulwich

DOCTOR EMMA'S REPLY: er...Yes.

Dear Vic

Here is my copy. Soz it's a bit late. Ran out of muses on the doctor emma one - perhaps you should write the rest of it. Do I get lots of money now?

If you want me to do some more, give us a ring.

Tell Sparks I'll marry him.

lots of

Emma x

E Freud.

UPPER-CLASS VOICES WITTERING. 'BOOBLE BOOBLE TAMPON...BOOBLE BOOBLE DARLINGS...BOOBLE BOOBLE IN THE AGA TRISTRAM...'

VLS *(shouts over FX)* You see what I mean? Not listening to a single word. They don't even realise they're on the radio. And when I shout louder, they just turn me down, they just turn me dow...

FX FADE VLS TO NOTHING. CUT TO CHAOTIC TRAFFIC SOUNDS.

VLS Suddenly, I find myself in Chaos. Chaos, fifty kilometres from Athens, is a small but totally disorganised Greek island in the Aegean. I decide to sample the local delicacies, and buy a delicious marinaded tape-wind on a skewer.

FX GREEK VOICE: 'YOU WANT CHILLI WITH YOUR TAPE-WIND?...OKAY, FIFTY DRACHMAS.' BOUZOUKI PLAYS, GRADUALLY SPEEDS UP AND BECOMES A TAPE-WIND.

VLS I digress. There is a very small minority of listeners who don't use Radio 4 as aural wallpaper. They are the ones who write the complaint letters. Let me explain in geriatric terms.

FX MUSIC *THE BODY IN QUESTION*.

VLS The listeners have an average age of a hundred and thirty-six, live in Harrogate or Eastbourne, still think that they're listening to the Home Service, and buy domestic lifts that slide up the bannisters, as advertised in the *Radio Times*. They write their complaint letters in wiggly handwriting on lined Basildon Bond writing paper, with an 'I am Able' address label stuck in the corner. For listeners who would like to know what goes on in their heads, here is a recording I prepared earlier of what goes on inside a Crumbly's brain.

FX SUBDUED THROBBING, HEARTBEAT. ARMY OFFICER VOICE: 'RIGHT, JOLLY GOOD. OKAY LEGS, IT'S HEADQUARTERS CORTICAL FUNCTION HERE. WOULD YOU PUSH THE ZIMMER FRAME OVER TO THE RADIO. RIGHT HANDS SWITCH ON *LOOSE ENDS*. GOOD. GRAB THE BASILDON BOND AND THE BIRO, IT'S AN UGLY PROGRAMME, THERE'S A LOT OF COMPLAINING TO DO. EARS, FILTER OUT EVERYTHING SAID EXCEPT THE SUGGESTIVE WORDS...'HIGH-PITCHED WHISTLE. 'WE'VE GOT SOME FEEDBACK ON THE DEAF AID, COULD YOU SORT THAT OUT? RIGHT, OFF WE GO.'

VOICE THROUGH RADIO, 'ZZZZZ... ZZZZZ.....NIPPLES....ZZZZ...ZZZ'

HQ VOICE: 'EARS, EARS...COULD YOU CONFIRM? DID HE JUST SAY NIPPLES?... RIGHT, WE'VE GOT HIM. HANDS, GET WRITING. "DEAR SIR, I SWITCHED OFF MY RADIO DISGUSTED..." NO, NO, DON'T *ACTUALLY* SWITCH OFF, WE LOVE IT REALLY. ANYWAY, CONTINUE WRITING. "THIS APPALLING FILTH SHOULD NOT BE ALLOWED...." ' SUBMARINE KLAXON. 'GOOD GOD, WHAT'S GOING ON?' PHONE RECEIVER LIFTED. 'HELLO, IT'S URETHRA HERE SIR. WE'VE GOT TROUBLE. WE'RE LOSING POWER. HIM ON THE RADIO, HE MENTIONED FOUNTAINS. WE CAN'T HOLD OUT.'

HQ VOICE: 'RIGHT, ACTION STATIONS. LEGS, GET YOURSELVES CROSSED.' URETHRA: 'IT'S TOO LATE SIR, WE'RE LOSING GALLONS BY THE MINUTE. WE'RE SINKING SIR, WE'RE SINKING....AAAARGGGH!' RUSHING WATER COVERS EVERYTHING. CUT.

VLS How do BBC producers deal with hate mail from Radio 4 Crumbly listeners?

FX TYPEWRITER SONG. TYPING. BBC PRODUCER DICTATING. 'OKAY, MISS UTTERSLAVE, TAKE A LETTER WILL YOU. DEAR MR CRUMBLY, THE BBC HAS BEEN RECEIVING A NUMBER OF DERANGED LETTERS, FULL OF HATE AND VENOM, FROM SOME LUNATIC. I'M SORRY TO SAY THAT HE HAS BEEN USING YOUR NAME AND ADDRESS. I

AM ENCLOSING A COPY OF THE LETTER. DO YOU RECOGNISE THE HANDWRITING? HAVE YOU ANY IDEA WHO THE MADMAN WRITING THIS UNHINGED FILTH MIGHT BE? I HAVE PASSED A COPY ON TO THE POLICE, WHO WILL DOUBTLESS WISH TO INTERVIEW YOU....' HYSTERICAL LAUGHTER.

VLS That is how we at the BBC deal with stroppy punters. Because frankly, shall I tell you what would suit us best at the BBC? You just listen to the radio, and keep your nasty little lined paper to yourself, okay? Patronising? That's right. Let me expound in condescending terms.

FX *THE BODY IN QUESTION.*

VLS Occasionally Radio 4 demeans itself by doing an Outside Broadcast and meeting the public. This could be from Ashby-de-la-Zouche or Millwall, but nine times out of ten it won't matter. It'll sound just the same. Crap. The producer and his entourage could have stayed in the studio in London and bunged on a few Sound Effects records. So why do they shell out all those extra mazoomas to go travelling? Is it because:

a) the heating at Broadcasting House has broken down again,

b) the landlord at the Three Tuns does the best venison in Windsor, or

c) the producer has a floozie, and has booked her into the Three Tuns for some cold, rubber insulated Programme Research?

FX SUDDEN CUT. SWINGLE SINGERS-STYLE SINGING.

VLS Suddenly, I grow a goatee beard, and a beret, and am hep, and have an inexplicable attack of the Swingles, and imagine myself to be Les Swingle, leader of the Les Swingle Singers.

FX SUDDEN CUT.

VLS Just time to have another gratuitous swipe at *Woman's Hour.* But don't worry, they don't mind, I'm in cahoots with the editor.

FX BAGPIPE MUSIC.

VLS Hello there. Well, I'm here in Cahoots, in Scotland, with the editor, and we've come here just to expedite that last pun. So it's over now to *Woman's Hour* coming live from Brixton, introduced by somebody very patronising indeed.

FX CROWD NOISE. BBC WOMAN PRESENTER: 'THANK YOU. NO, THE WORD IS MATRONISING, IF YOU DON'T MIND. WELL, WE'RE OUT AND ABOUT TODAY IN BRIXTON WITH SOME BLACK PEOPLE. COULD I ASK YOU SIR... SOMEONE AT THE BBC TOLD ME THAT ALL YOU JIVE MOTHERS LIKE TO ROLL YOUR EYES AND SING OL' MAN RIBBER. IS THAT AN OVER-SIMPLIFICATION OF WEST INDIAN CULTURE AT ALL?...OH DEAR, THAT'S ALL WE'VE GOT TIME FOR, SO I'VE WRITTEN SOME SPECIAL WOMAN'S HOUR LYRICS FOR A LOCAL BAND WITH US TODAY CALLED HAILI GANJA. SO, TAKE IT AWAY, FELLAS.' REGGAE BACKTRACK. WEST INDIAN VOICE SINGS:
    ME GOT ME KNITTIN PATTERN,
    ME GOT ME DISCHARGE.
    ME GOT ME JENNY MURRAY.
    ME MAKIN DAMSON JAM,
    ME TALK ABOUT DE DISCHARGE,
    LET ME TALK ABOUT DE DISCHARGE...
    AN TING.

FX SNAP. SILENCE. TRICKLE OF GREEN SLIME.

VLS Oh Lummy! I've broken it, I've broken Radio 4. The Controller, Miss Howard, told me that if I played with it too much it would break. Now she'll get jolly baity and smack the backs of my legs until they're red raw. Oh cripes, Great Timothy, please Ned, don't let her slap the backs of my legs, otherwise I'll tell Esther Rantzen about our little secret, how you made me kiss Punch goodnight. Oh dear, oh no....

FX SLAPPING.

VLS Oh no, she's slapping them, oh, boo hoo, *(completely deadpan),* oh, boo hoo, the end.... the end.

BROADCAST...
TELEPHONE 01-580 4468 TELEX...
EGRAMS AND CABLES: BROADCASTS LONDON TELEX

Dear Mr. Gorbachev,

I contacted 'London Management', (they deal with all the greats: Bobby Crush, Reg Varney and even, I think in the past, Winifred Atwell, who is Winifred Notwell these days - excuse my little English joke!). Anyhow chuck, they said that they did not represent you, and that I should go through your agents at the Kremlin. Speaking of the Kremlin, my concierge Mrs Tribly went on an Intasun package tour to Moscow and couldn't resist standing by the main entrance and shouting 'is Len in?'. This is another example of the famous British sense of humour - do they have a sense of humour in Russia too? However, when I did eventually get through to the Kremlin, and asked to speak to an agent, I was given short shrift and more than a mouthful of Borsch tongue sandwich from the retarded malchick operating your telephones there. I am firm. Very firm.

I am a regular presenter on the very excellent socialist BBC Radio 4 programme, "Loose Ends". And I am firm. Yes indeed, I am firm. At the moment, I'm trying to arrange a regular, light hearted feature called 'In the not fully qualified but I've read a lot about it psychiatrist's chair', in which, disguising my voice to sound high-pitched and Irish, I ask guests certain searing questions in a no-messing pertinacious manner. Already in the can is my 13 minute interview with the somewhat gauche socialist, Michael Foot in which, shortly before he stormed out, I said that his attire made Worzel Gummidge look like Man at C & A. Don't get me wrong, I don't merely interview socialists; last week, for example, I gave Thora Hird the twice over vis-a-vis secret membership of the Ku Klux Klan.

Pol Pot has been booked, along with Reagan. It's a big series - we've got a big budget. You are a man with a story to tell. A charming wife. You're the salt of the earth and you know which wronguns to send off and mine it. Mrs. Thatcher's daughter, my wife Carol, will be happy to attend to your every whim should you require anything 'extra'. In the meantime, the programme I'm thinking about is SATURDAY OCT 17th AT 10 O CLOCK, 1987.

If this is no good for you, do let me know. But please, please let me know BEFORE the day, otherwise we'll have 10 minutes dead air on our hands, and that leaves R4 continuity announcers more time to ramble under the influence of that horrid crack M.Howard is passing round in the canteen.

I think you are a leader of immense strength and a world saviour. God bless you and RSVP. Your greatest English fan,

VICTOR LEWis smith

Victor Lewis Smith Room 7076

Trying to be Henry Root, part V
(I give up).

BRITISH
BROAD... ...RATION
TELEGRAMS AND ...ON W1A 1AA
...0 4468 TELEX: 265781
BROADCASTS LONDON TELEX

Your Holyness,

May I start by being a little familiar? I very much enjoyed your show — "Urbi et Orbi" on the tv last Easter. But you'll laugh when I tell you that I tuned in expecting some sort of Welsh comedy duo the likes of the late great "Ronny e Ryan"!

A few years ago, my concierge Mrs Tribly told me that you visited my beautiful city of York. Then, you did us the honour of kissing the sod. I know the feeling. I've done a bit of that myself, but as I said to I magistrati at the time, "I thought the boy was my sister and was overcome with the heatstroke your Honour!".

Your Holyness, In short, it's great to be alive and it's even greater to have a sense of humour! You're a great guy. I know you understand that. I am firm. Very firm.

Would you please appear on my programme, "Loose Ends", on BBC Radio 4, England? The critics in their usual harsh way have said the programme is a little like 'being born dead with cancer', but you know what critics are like when you're trying to tackle serious issues. Prime Minister Thatcher's daughter is a regular on the programmme. I thought I should tell you that in case you thought you were dealing with some sub-hospital radio toot.

I've provisionally booked you in for SAT 17th OCT AT 10 AM. Please let me know if that is a problem.

Pax vobiscum,

VICTOR Lewis-Smith

Victor Lewis Smith. Room 7076

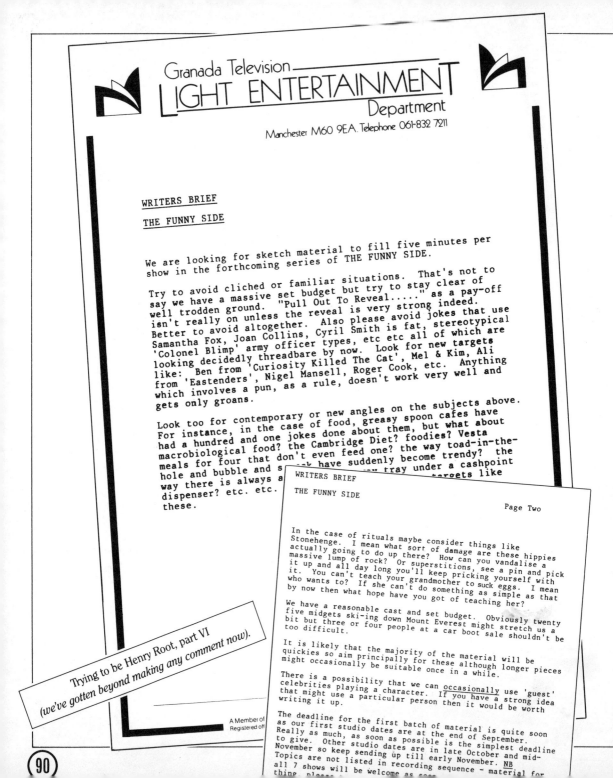

Granada Television

LIGHT ENTERTAINMENT
Department

Manchester M60 9EA. Telephone 061-832 7211

WRITERS BRIEF

THE FUNNY SIDE

We are looking for sketch material to fill five minutes per
show in the forthcoming series of THE FUNNY SIDE.

Try to avoid cliched or familiar situations. That's not to
say we have a massive set budget but try to stay clear of
well trodden ground. "Pull Out To Reveal....." as a pay-off
isn't really on unless the reveal is very strong indeed.
Better to avoid altogether. Also please avoid jokes that use
Samantha Fox, Joan Collins, Cyril Smith is fat, stereotypical
'Colonel Blimp' army officer types, etc etc all of which are
looking decidedly threadbare by now. Look for new targets
like: Ben from 'Curiosity Killed The Cat', Mel & Kim, Ali
from 'Eastenders', Nigel Mansell, Roger Cook, etc. Anything
which involves a pun, as a rule, doesn't work very well and
gets only groans.

Look too for contemporary or new angles on the subjects above.
For instance, in the case of food, greasy spoon cafes have
had a hundred and one jokes done about them, but what about
macrobiological food? the Cambridge Diet? foodies? Vesta
meals for four that don't even feed one? the way toad-in-the-
hole and bubble and s???? have ??? ??? tray under a cashpoint
way there is always a ??? ?????? ??? ??????s like
dispenser? etc. etc. ???
these.

WRITERS BRIEF

THE FUNNY SIDE

Page Two

In the case of rituals maybe consider things like
Stonehenge. I mean what sort of damage are these hippies
actually going to do up there? How can you vandalise a
massive lump of rock? Or superstitions, see a pin and pick
it up and all day long you'll keep pricking yourself with
it. You can't teach your grandmother to suck eggs. I mean
who wants to? If she can't do something as simple as that
by now then what hope have you got of teaching her?

We have a reasonable cast and set budget. Obviously twenty
five midgets ski-ing down Mount Everest might stretch us a
bit but three or four people at a car boot sale shouldn't be
too difficult.

It is likely that the majority of the material will be
quickies so aim principally for these although longer pieces
might occasionally be suitable once in a while.

There is a possibility that we can occasionally use 'guest'
celebrities playing a character. If you have a strong idea
that might use a particular person then it would be worth
writing it up.

The deadline for the first batch of material is quite soon
as our first studio dates are at the end of September.
Really as much, as soon as possible is the simplest deadline
to give. Other studio dates are in late October and mid-
November so keep sending up till early November. NB
Topics are not listed in recording sequence - material for
all 7 shows will be welcome as soon ???
thing ???

Trying to be Henry Root, part VI
(we've gotten beyond making any comment now).

A Member of
Registered off

THE FUNNY SIDE ABOUT FUNERALS

FUN AT THE CREM:

Outside shot of a crematorium with a coffin being carried in through the door. Babs Windsor slips on a stray pilchard (close up) what has fallen from Mick Miller's sandwich and slides on her bum while her dress gets caught and the front rips off.

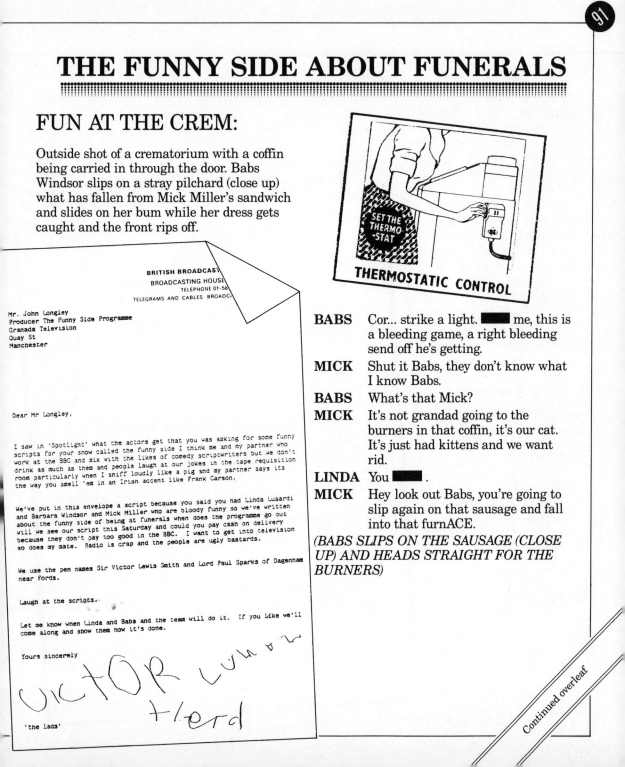

SET THE THERMO-STAT

THERMOSTATIC CONTROL

BRITISH BROADCAST
BROADCASTING HOUSE
TELEPHONE 01-58
TELEGRAMS AND CABLES BROADC

Mr. John Longley
Producer The Funny Side Programme
Granada Television
Quay St
Manchester

Dear Mr Longley,

I saw in 'Spotlight' what the actors get that you was asking for some funny scripts for your show called the funny side I think me and my partner who work at the BBC and mix with the likes of comedy scriptwriters but we don't drink as much as them and people laugh at our jokes in the tape requisition room particularly when I sniff loudly like a pig and my partner says its the way you smell 'em in an Irish accent like Frank Carson.

We've put in this envelope a script because you said you had Linda Lusardi and Barbara Windsor and Mick Miller who are bloody funny so we've written about the funny side of being at funerals when does the programme go out will we see our script this Saturday and could you pay casn on delivery because they don't pay too good in the BBC. I want to get into television so does my mate. Radio is crap and the people are ugly bastards.

We use the pen names Sir Victor Lewis Smith and Lord Paul Sparks of Dagenham near Fords.

Laugh at the scripts.

Let me know when Linda and Babs and the team will do it. If you like we'll come along and show them how it's done.

Yours sincerely

VICTOR LEWIS
+Lord

'the lads'

BABS	Cor... strike a light. ▮▮▮ me, this is a bleeding game, a right bleeding send off he's getting.
MICK	Shut it Babs, they don't know what I know Babs.
BABS	What's that Mick?
MICK	It's not grandad going to the burners in that coffin, it's our cat. It's just had kittens and we want rid.
LINDA	You ▮▮▮▮.
MICK	Hey look out Babs, you're going to slip again on that sausage and fall into that furnACE.

(BABS SLIPS ON THE SAUSAGE (CLOSE UP) AND HEADS STRAIGHT FOR THE BURNERS)

Continued overleaf

BABS   Ooooooooooo errrrrrrrr lumeeeeeeeeee christ almighty, I like it warm but ▓▓▓ this for a game of ▓▓▓▓▓▓▓ * soldiers.

(BABS IS TURNED TO ASH)

MUSIC THAT GOES: DA DSA DA DA DEE DEE DEE DUM DEE DEE DE DIDDLE DIDDLE DUM DUM WAH WAH WAH!

CLOSE UP SHOT OF MICK AND LINDA LUSARDI HOLDING THE ASHTRAY WITH A PAIR OF HEAVILY MADE UP GLASS EYES AND SOME ASH

LINDA   She's not much to look at these days is she?

MICK   Yep. It just goes to show smoking can ruin your health.

AUDIENCE LAUGHTER (NO NEED TO DUB IT ON. IT'S A STRONG ONE THIS).

THE END.

*If the language is a bit too strong you can put the words rotten old and bother instead of ▓▓▓▓▓▓ or ▓▓▓▓ .
OK?

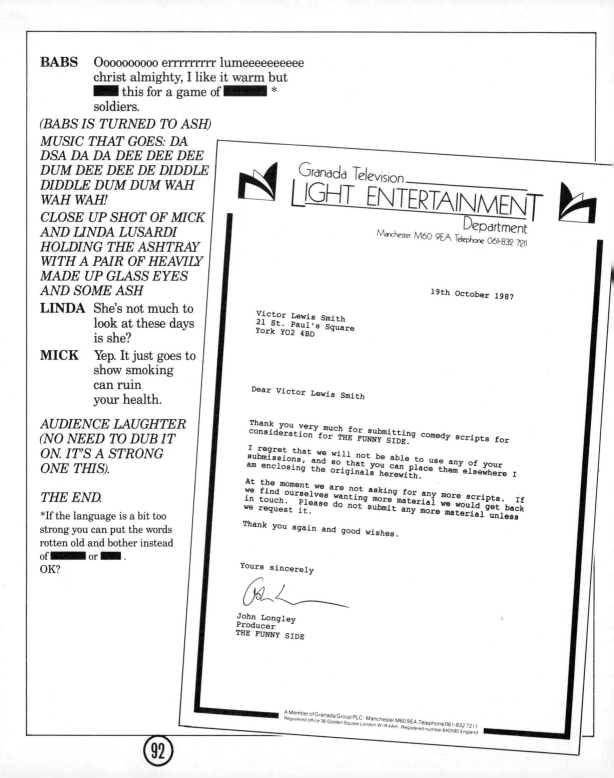

Granada Television

LIGHT ENTERTAINMENT
Department

Manchester M60 9EA. Telephone 061-832 7211

19th October 1987

Victor Lewis Smith
21 St. Paul's Square
York YO2 4BD

Dear Victor Lewis Smith

Thank you very much for submitting comedy scripts for consideration for THE FUNNY SIDE.

I regret that we will not be able to use any of your submissions, and so that you can place them elsewhere I am enclosing the originals herewith.

At the moment we are not asking for any more scripts. If we find ourselves wanting more material we would get back in touch. Please do not submit any more material unless we request it.

Thank you again and good wishes.

Yours sincerely

John Longley
Producer
THE FUNNY SIDE

A Member of Granada Group PLC - Manchester M60 9EA. Telephone 061-832 7211
Registered office 36 Golden Square London W1 R 4AH · Registered number 840590 England

Carol Thatcher

Mr Gardhouse had one of his characteristic brainwaves for my first *Loose Ends* assignment — Thatcher off to the tip. It was to do a tough, investigative six-minute item on garbology (the science of trash, garbage, rubbish, call it what you will).

It all came about because of a minor

Following hard on the heels of that inaugural contribution to Ned's Saturday morning slot on the Beeb I've done a variety of other off-beat little assignments including *Loose Ends* first underwater interview, bobsleighing, shoplifting, learning to hot air balloon with the man who taught Richard Branson and a guest appearance as a cheerleader with the LA Rams.

On being a *Loose Ends* reporter

sensation in the national press concerning some kids who'd found a finger on a tip down near Bristol. One pathologist said it was a human finger but a second opinion changed that to a rubber finger. Disappointing. Wielding a microphone, I sought out the licensed totter in search of fingers and other 'finds'.

He said it was the filthiest job in the world. The incentive? 'Hopefully we'll find something one day and be able to retire.' Presumably not fingers.

What sort of a comment did he think the junk the locals brought to the tip was on civilisation in Richmond? 'They're a load of wasters.'

The underwater number required me to present myself at a posh Knightsbridge health club and submerge self (now in swim-suit) in swimming pool for an underwater serenade on the saxophone by Peter Thomas of Deep Sea Jiving. Quite a novel experience apart from nearly drowning. But my in-depth questions in the shallow end made no headway through the chlorinated gallons in between interviewer and interviewee so we surfaced (CT's sole effort ever at being upwardly mobile).

Does anything else sound like a saxophone underwater or is it a uniquely refined, pure musical experience? Well, according to Peter Thomas whales sound fairly similar.

93

And on the listening front let me also tell you about the talking budgie quest starring Great Britain's chattiest Joeys. It was in Birmingham. I discovered that talkative owners have talkative birds. Some, alas, were overcome with stage fright and wouldn't utter a word, but I was impressed by one with a flair for languages which banged away in Japanese. I won't make a budgie judge, though.

'Is this Miss World?' I inquired, admiring a rather fetching species.
'No. It's Mr Universe,' corrected a high flyer bird buff.

My next 'sound' assignment was in the gents down in the basement of Broadcasting House. Mr Gardhouse had noticed that a west country male choir was offering to audition aspiring choristers in the privacy of their own bathrooms so an opera singer, the Master of Choirs at King's School, Canterbury, Barry Rose and I had a rendezvous in the loos to assess the acoustics.

Don't laugh, bathrooms and tube stations really are the best places if you want your voice to sound like you've always dreamed. I was rather pleased with this item but Ned doesn't waste any time deflating the puffed up egos of purring presenters. 'Carol Thatcher going down the plughole with a load of bathroom baritones,' was Ned's line to finish my piece back in the studio.

When the LA Rams came to Wembley to pit their skills against fellow American footballers, the Denver Broncos, they brought their very own cheerleading squad and I went along to find out exactly what was involved in becoming a high kicking, ring-of-confidence-smiling, tanned, toned dancing, chanting Barbie doll clone. My pom-pom routine was a messy disaster (absolutely no co-ordination or style), but I had hopes that my Cheshire Cat grin smile might pass. No, not a chance. 'It's too stressed out,' the champ cheerleader in charge of try-outs (United States-ese for auditions) informed me. Too what?

Cancel trip to California. But I did get through international departures once to sample the bone rattling dangers of the bobsleigh track in Cervinia, Italy, where the British team was competing in the European Championships. Helmet on, strapped into a four-man bob, poised to commentate as *Loose Ends* winter sports correspondent we hurtled into a white vortex with G-force and steep curves. At the end I managed to gasp: 'I feel like scrambled eggs.' I did and even Curva Bianca which I fancied might be a soothing aperitif had turned out to be another blessed bend in the ice tunnel.

I'm not the only Thatcher on the show: Mum keeps on cropping up in Victor Lewis Smith's monologue and *Loose Ends* covered my twin brother's wedding. That week, in my capacity as sister of the bridegroom, I went off to the Bride and Home Exhibition in Alexandra Palace. There, I discovered love bags of herbs and essential oils which induce warmth of spirit and pleasing thoughts. Just the thing for newlyweds and they came with practical advice from the salesperson: 'I do strongly recommend that you never have the sleep mix and the love mix in the same room because it can lead to certain problems...' This I passed on to bridegroom and bride, Mark and Diane.

The *Loose Ends* DO-IT-YOURSELF NOTTING HILL CARNIVAL KIT

O.K. So it wasn't every day of the week you wanted to wake up to a front garden full of empty Red Stripe cans. Course not. But it was the Carnival, wasn't it? And it only happened once a year. And even if it did take the Borough of Kensington & Chelsea the next eleven months to clear it all up, it was worth it wasn't it? Course it was.

But there's been some talk of banning it. And just because (last year) some guy got stabbed to death overcharging for a can of Coca-Cola.

Well now. Just in case the boys in blue down the Notting Hill nick decide to Tippex this multi-racial, multi-cultural évènement out of the Caribbean end of Kensington's social calendar, the *Loose Ends* team has come up with a Do-it-yourself-Carnival-Kit. This kit comprises everything you will need for a truly walk-good, cool-running carnival in the comfort of your very own home. All you have to do is send a cheque or postal order for £450 to our brilliantly innovative and creative producer, the nice Mr. Gardhouse, (c/o 'The George'), and you too can experience a right-on, no-problem Bank Holiday event.

Your luxury Carnival kit will include:

1. A six-pack of CRUCIAL BREW (the 180% proof equivalent of Red Stripe).
2. One Vidal Sassoon dreadlock wig (or you could always try using his shampoo).
3. One Tam (yellow and green) for keeping your Vidal Sassoon dreadlock wig in.
4. One volume of Linton Quasi Johnson's *Collected Soaca Poetry*. (You remember him. The one Trinity College Cambridge turned down for a fellowship, on the grounds that he was neither a known KGB agent, nor a practising homosexual.)
5. One 'Best of Bob Marley and the Wailers' tape.
6. One ghetto blaster.
7. One portion of saltfish and ackee.
8. One portion of calalloo.
9. One portion of jerk chicken.
10. One portion of goat curry.
11. One portion of Mannish water (interesting soup with a bull's ▬▬▬ in the bottom. If you don't eat it all up, you don't get any afters).
12. One booklet full of Michael Manley promises (for wiping up purposes).

VAT, postage and packing included. Stay Cool!

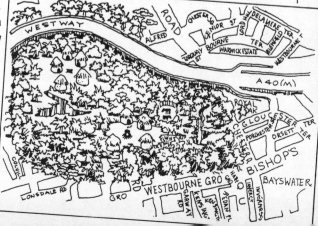

Engineers' Corner

A guide for those technical minded readers who want to know just how the BBC Boffins and Management arrange for Ned Sherrin's use of the word 'thelerethism' on *Loose Ends* to come out of your transistor radios.

Pork Packer, fuck the parson, those fleshy gibbosites, Millican and Nesbit, belch on a velch......

thelerethism

Even at this very primary stage, BBC microphones are designed to filter out any unsavoury phrases or words which might offend any member of the Radio 4 audience. 'Thelerethism' gets through the net.

1887. The BBC sends young Nedward Sherrin to Reith College Oxford where he is taught long words which will confuse and delight his audience in years to come.

At precisely 10.36 and 23″ on Nedwin builds up 250 lb per cubic foot of pressure in his diaphragm (equal to 20 calories, equal to $\frac{1}{2}$ of a Weetabix eaten during a substantial BBC breakfast) and releases the word 'THELERETHISM' from his throat at a steady speed of 127 m.p.h. The word hits the microphone EXACTLY 1 nanno second after.

theleret

Half a Weetabix

Nedward gains a BA in Chat Shows (Hons) and after postgraduate study into the third BBC Time Pip is interviewed by a BBC board for the position of anchorman on *LOOSE ENDS*.

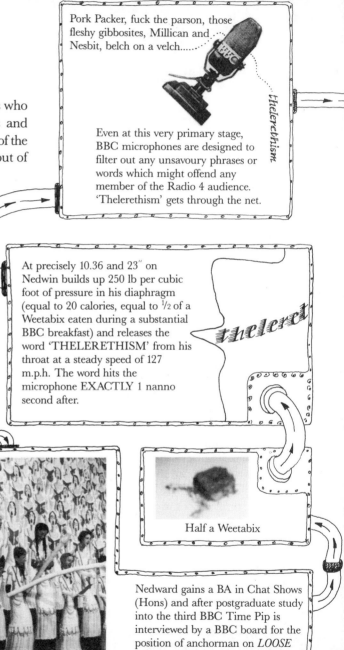

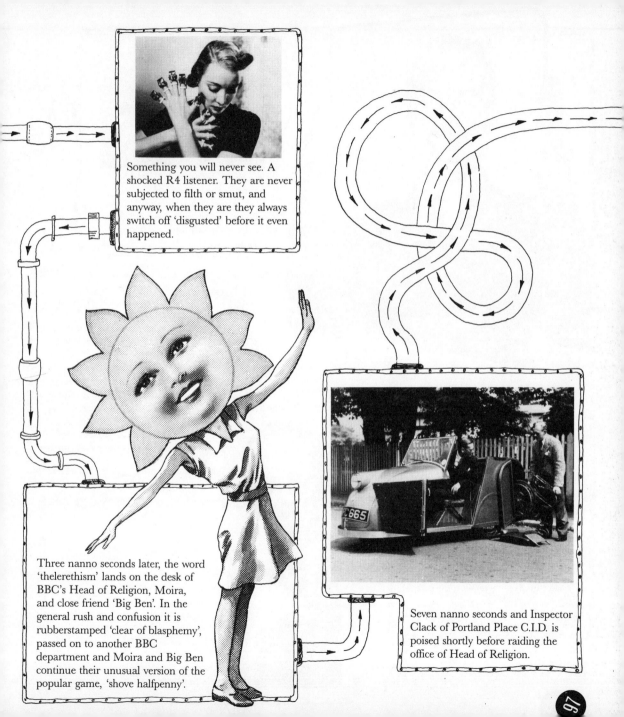

Something you will never see. A shocked R4 listener. They are never subjected to filth or smut, and anyway, when they are they always switch off 'disgusted' before it even happened.

Three nanno seconds later, the word 'thelerethism' lands on the desk of BBC's Head of Religion, Moira, and close friend 'Big Ben'. In the general rush and confusion it is rubberstamped 'clear of blasphemy', passed on to another BBC department and Moira and Big Ben continue their unusual version of the popular game, 'shove halfpenny'.

Seven nanno seconds and Inspector Clack of Portland Place C.I.D. is poised shortly before raiding the office of Head of Religion.

At exactly 10.36 and 23″ and 58 nanno seconds the word 'thelerethism' spurts out of a wireless in Orpington and hits the eardrums of Mr and Mrs Doris and Arthur Twinkle.

Thirty-six nanno seconds and it's 'lift off' for Nedwin's plucky little four syllable utterance. It's 27 miles to Orpington at 186,000 ½ miles per second. Meanwhile, realising that they are 'bang to rights', the Head of Religion and 'Big Ben' decide that the courts of law are not for them and take the fast route from the seventh floor to the ground via the head of a BBC Security man, who, minding his own business, joins them on a journey even further than Orpington.

Nine nanno seconds on and the Chairman of the BBC, Mr. Marmalade Butty, is interrupted during his eight hour stint as Test Card Girl. He is shown the word 'thelerethism' on his autocue. Should he as much as wink one eye or even slightly twitch the string of his balloons, the use of the word 'thelerethism' will be banned from transmission on *Loose Ends*. As it is, the Chairman gives it the thumbs up and continues with his part time modelling job, remaining quite still until, five hours later, when the live orchestra plays its final cadence and the test card director shouts 'OK boys, it's a rap'.

Thirteen nanno seconds and the word 'thelerethism' is given a final examination by the BBC's one-fingered gynaecologist before embarking on the long journey from Broadcasting House to a transistor radio in Orpington.

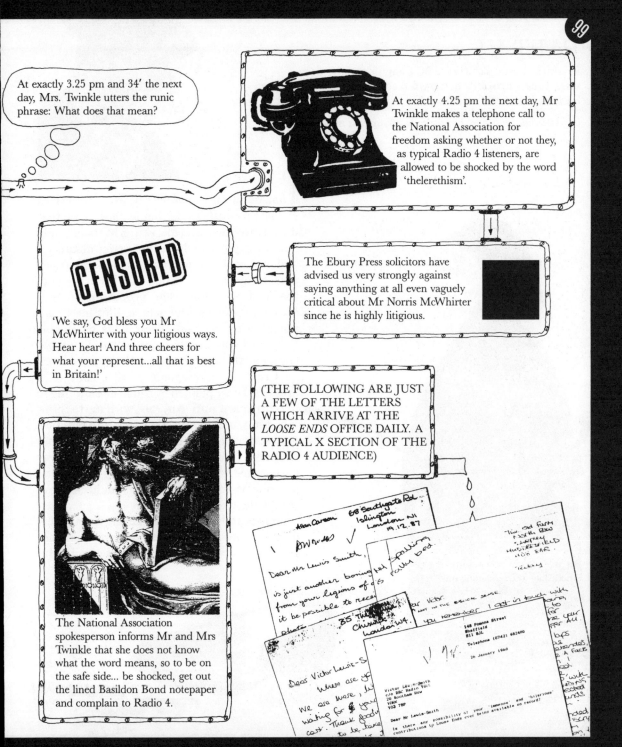

At exactly 3.25 pm and 34′ the next day, Mrs. Twinkle utters the runic phrase: What does that mean?

At exactly 4.25 pm the next day, Mr Twinkle makes a telephone call to the National Association for freedom asking whether or not they, as typical Radio 4 listeners, are allowed to be shocked by the word 'thelerethism'.

CENSORED

'We say, God bless you Mr McWhirter with your litigious ways. Hear hear! And three cheers for what your represent...all that is best in Britain!'

The Ebury Press solicitors have advised us very strongly against saying anything at all even vaguely critical about Mr Norris McWhirter since he is highly litigious.

(THE FOLLOWING ARE JUST A FEW OF THE LETTERS WHICH ARRIVE AT THE *LOOSE ENDS* OFFICE DAILY. A TYPICAL X SECTION OF THE RADIO 4 AUDIENCE)

The National Association spokesperson informs Mr and Mrs Twinkle that she does not know what the word means, so to be on the safe side... be shocked, get out the lined Basildon Bond notepaper and complain to Radio 4.

PART VI

in which Harold Coaltart, BBC Commissionaire does
something with a PP3 battery, a piece of string, and the wiggly
bit from his aunt's hearing aid

(it's not that amusing, but we're working to a deadline)

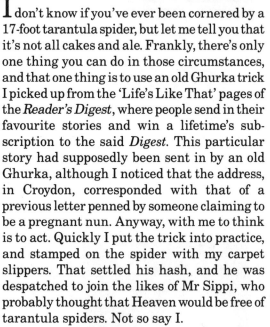

I don't know if you've ever been cornered by a 17-foot tarantula spider, but let me tell you that it's not all cakes and ale. Frankly, there's only one thing you can do in those circumstances, and that one thing is to use an old Ghurka trick I picked up from the 'Life's Like That' pages of the *Reader's Digest*, where people send in their favourite stories and win a lifetime's subscription to the said *Digest*. This particular story had supposedly been sent in by an old Ghurka, although I noticed that the address, in Croydon, corresponded with that of a previous letter penned by someone claiming to be a pregnant nun. Anyway, with me to think is to act. Quickly I put the trick into practice, and stamped on the spider with my carpet slippers. That settled his hash, and he was despatched to join the likes of Mr Sippi, who probably thought that Heaven would be free of tarantula spiders. Not so say I.

Immediately I set to work rifling through his drawers, on the look-out for any personal possessions which might suit my own life-in-

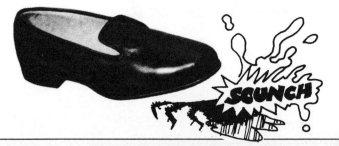

the-fast-lane life style. And what a strange collection of bits of toot I uncovered in that Aladdin's Cave de la Sippi, pardon my French: a glass tube attached to a rubber suction bulb, 15,000 copies of *Health and Efficiency* magazine dating back to the early 1950s, an old and well-thumbed copy of the Dicky Valentine fanzine in which was written a note in childish handwriting about blackmail being an ugly word, a pamphlet on gentlemen's stylish rubber underwear, a leaflet entitled 'Repatriation Now', a knitting pattern for a posing pouch, something I cannot describe because the acid from the batteries had mutilated the plastic, sheet music for numerous hits by Pearl Carr and Teddy Johnson, in particular a song called 'Sing Little Birdy', a bung of some sort, a book called *Knowledge For The Growing Boy*, a Fireball XL5 annual signed by the man who composed the theme tune for the series, a Mr Barry Grey, two tubes of ointment, some sacking containing a shrunken skull, marked 'A Present From the Philippines', a telegram from someone called Bobby claiming that bunnies can and will go to Paris, 15 Polaroid pictures of what looked like the inside of someone's mouth with the teeth removed, a monocle, a packet of

bird seed which claimed to make your budgie bounce with health, a woggle, a threatening letter, a clip-on hairy chest, a set of eyebrow tweezers in mother-of-pearl, an artist's impression signed 'Sippi' of a naked Mohammed Ali, a small black book with a variety of telephone numbers, some marked with a tick and 'Job Done' written by them, a plaster cast to fit around an arm, a harmonica, a hair shirt, some ropes and pulleys, a hangman's noose, a tawse, a jamboree bag, a gross of Lemsip packets, some white powder in small plastic bags, a bottle of linseed oil, a box of indoor fireworks, a signed photograph of the zany radio presenter Richard Baker, a transcript of a court case involving Mr Baker, a copy of *Goat Farmer's Monthly* magazine, a black balaclava helmet, a sawn-off shotgun, five books of Green Shield Stamps, a personal massage kit, a book of cloakroom tickets, some balloons, a pair of binoculars with 'Do Not Remove From This Theatre' on them, two tickets for the show *Oh, Calcutta* and a box of matches.

Frankly, I was disgusted. Any man who could leave a box of matches lying around where young children might get their hands on them deserves a sound thrashing. Straight away, I went down to Brenda and said, Brenda, I said, we are LEAVING NOW. And it was as we were walking up our pathway that I noticed that the bedroom lights were on. I said to Brenda, did you leave the bedroom lights on Moggy? Electricity doesn't grow on trees you know my girl. Anyway, cut a long story short, Brenda said she hadn't left them on, and since Wayne and Tracy were on a camping holiday together, I feared the worst ... we had been invaded by squatters.

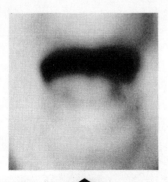

For legal reasons, this picture is uncaptioned.

Has the Coaltart household been squatted in? Turn to p.118 to find out.

Here is a boy scout. He is Jimmy. Look! He is wearing a smart uniform with a leather woggle around his neck. Look at his garters. They are holding up his stockings. His leather shoes are very very shiny. He is saluting the scout troop leader, a much older boy. He respects and looks up to his scout troop leader. It is bob-a-job week soon. There will be lots of polishing and grass to cut. There will be a big jamboree at the end of bob-a-job week. Jimmy has been promised a look at his scout leader's collection of fine shells collected on Frinton beach. Look! Jimmy is smiling! He is happy!

The BBC and the murphia

VLS You may remember that last week I broke Radio 4, and received a thorough wigging and detention from Mr Checkland. I spent most of the week picking up the bits with Harold Coaltart, the BBC Commissionaire.

FX GLASS BREAKING, RUBBISH BEING SWEPT. COALTART: 'LOOK AT THE BLEEDING MESS YOU'VE CAUSED, LOOK, RADIO 4, IT'S ALMOST BRAND NEW, I MEAN, WHAT A WASTE. LOOK AT THAT, I MEAN THE MAINSPRING'S GONE ON THE SHIPPING FORECAST, LOOK THE CROMARTY'S BURNT OUT...'

FX VLS: 'NO, LICK OF PAINT...GOOD AS NEW...' SPRING BOIINGS.
COALTART: 'DON'T KNOW 'BOUT GOOD AS NEW, HERE, PASS OVER THOSE BITS OF MARGARET HOWARD.'
VLS: 'OH LOOK, THE HEAD'S STILL WORKING.'
MARGARET HOWARD: 'HELLO AGAIN, HELLO AGAIN, HELLO AGAIN...'
COALTART: 'NO, I DON'T LIKE IT, IT GIVES ME THE WILLIES, I DON'T LIKE IT WITH THE HEAD OFF.'

FX CUT TO *SAILING BY* PLAYING UNEVENLY.

VLS It's my own fault, they told me but I would not listen. I fiddled with Radio 4 so much that the Bakelite snapped, and green stuff came out. *Sailing By* is warped, *Does He Take Sugar?* is no more than a sea of twisted chrome, and the transmitters have become so weak that the Long Wave has been invaded by Warsaw Radio so, from now on, Jenny Murray is likely to have a bit of Pole in her.

FX WOMAN SHRIEKS.

VLS As a result of my wickedness in Big School, the Head of House, Mr Marmalade Butty, stops my pocket money and I find myself in penury.

FX TUBE STATION ATMOSPHERE. TANNOY 'THIS TRAIN TERMINATES HERE.'

VLS You'll find Penury on the Northern Line, change at Waterloo. If you're insolvent, you have to change first at Newbury Park.

FX TANNOY 'MIND THE GAP.' CUT. PAUL TEMPLE THEME, SOUNDS OF HAMMERING.

VLS I board the train, leaving a small knothole for the driver to see through.

FX CUT TO DOG HOWLING.

VLS Back in the flat I switch on the fictional whippet, which, after much struggling, serious fictional mutilation, and fictional amputation of the back legs, and fictionally ripping out its tongue which I do fictionally, just to annoy dog lovers and the RSPCA, I have converted into an attractive and fetching lampshade, and that will teach it to get more famous than me, will it not?

FX PHONE RINGS.

VLS Oh, I should say 'There goes the phone' now.

FX LIFTS RECEIVER.

VLS: Ah, it's the nice Mr Gardhouse...hello Mr Gardhouse...he is depressed, he is in a state of Catatonia...Why are you in a state of Catatonia the nice Mr Gardhouse?...You're paying homage?...what, to Catatonia?...well, I never... *(close mike)* Catatonia, somewhere on the Iberian Peninsula, is where Mr Gardhouse has been exiled as the man ultimately responsible for my breaking Radio 4 *(into phone)*...Anyway, what's cooking baby, as they say at *Woman's Hour?*...Going to be re-educated by the BBC?...what, me?...they're going to make me

nice?...where's the BBC going to send me?...
You'll give me a clue?...

FX   GARDHOUSE SINGS 'THE IRISH
     WASHERWOMAN' DOWN PHONE. CUT.
     FIDDLE PLAYING 'THE IRISH
     WASHERWOMAN.' SHOUTING.

VLS I find myself in culcated. Culcated is a small
     village on the outskirts of County Mayo, at a
     secret underground BBC Irish Charm School.
     I'm being instructed in how to be a likeable
     Media Personality. Let me explain in pedagogical
     terms.

FX   *THE BODY IN QUESTION* MUSIC.

VLS At the very centre of the BBC is a group of
     vacuous but ultra-charming professional Irish
     persons. This benign cosa nostra is known in the
     media as 'the Murphia,' and includes the likes
     of yer Terry Wogan, yer Henry Kelly, yer Gloria
     Hunniford and yer Frank Delaney. The British
     public love to hear charming Irish blarney and
     well-groomed Irishmen who say 'Desist, me
     hearties' with an impish grin while waggling their
     bodies from side to side. Here is a recording of
     what's happening between their ears while they
     are exuding their blarney.

FX   5'' TOTAL SILENCE.

VLS No cerebral activity, no alpha, no beta wave at
     all. Nothing. But BBC rubber executives prefer
     smarm to grey matter, for, as the Latin motto
     above Broadcasting House says, 'Nemo anum
     sapientum amat' or, in English, 'No one loves a
     smartarse'. I am forced to take a crash course in
     BBC smarm.

FX   FIDDLE MUSIC. NONE-TOO-CONVINCING
     IRISH VOICE: 'OKAY CHAPS, SETTLE
     DOWN NOW. I'M BBC HEAD OF IRISH
     BLARNEY. SO, YOU HAVE YOUR MAPS
     OF THE LONDON UNDERGROUND, TV
     CENTRE'S MARKED WITH AN 'X', SURE
     AND I'M STARTING TO LOSE MY
     ACCENT BEJABERS, SO... (ACCENT
     SLIPS GRADUALLY INTO BBC HOME
     COUNTIES) ...GET YOUR GLYCERINE
     EYEDROPS FOR THE AUTHENTIC
     IRISH TWINKLE, AND REPEAT AFTER

ME 'SURE, DANNY BOY, DOESN'T ME
MOTHER'S BLUE EYES SHINE LIKE
THE DERRY DEW ME HEARTIES, AND
I'D LIKE SIX HUNDRED THOUSAND
POUNDS FOR NEXT YEAR'S CONTRACT
MR GRADE, AND HOW'S SHE CUTTIN'?'.

FX   RECRUITS REPEAT CUT.

VLS I graduate with First Class honours in Applied
     Smarm, shave my head, change my name to Al
     O'Pecia, and am instantly offered a vacuous chat
     show. On my way home, I call in at my local
     corner shop.

FX   SHOP DOORBELL RINGS.
     VLS: 'HELLO, I'D LIKE TO BUY FOUR
     CORNERS PLEASE.'
     SHOPKEEPER: 'CERTAINLY SIR. HOBBY
     OF YOURS, IS IT SIR?'
     VLS: 'YES. I LIKE MAKING ROUND
     THINGS SQUARE.'
     SHOPKEEPER: 'I SEE. ANYTHING ELSE
     SIR?'
     VLS: 'YES, SOME ANADIN. I HAVE A
     HEADACHE...NO, ON SECOND
     THOUGHTS, I'LL HAVE NOTHING.'
     SHOPKEEPER: 'AND WHY IS THAT SIR?'
     VLS: 'BECAUSE NOTHING ACTS FASTER
     THAN ANADIN.'
     SHOPKEEPER: 'OH, I SEE SIR, VERY
     RISIBLE. DIDN'T DO SO WELL WITH
     THE IRISH ACCENT IN THE LAST
     SCENE THOUGH, DID WE?'
     VLS: 'I'M SORRY, I WAS FROM MY
     MOTHER'S WOMB UNTIMELY RIP'T.
     AND I'LL THANK YOU TO FIRMLY
     KEEP YOUR MOUTH SHUT.'

FX   SOUND OF CLOTH RIPPING.

VLS I split my infinitives and leave. Back in the flat,
     I tune in the radio to hear myself choose eight
     Desert Island Discs for Mr Parkinson.

FX   PARKINSON: 'LET'S HAVE ANOTHER
     CHOICE OF RECORD'.
     VLS: 'IT'S ANOTHER SOUND EFFECT
     RECORD MICHAEL, THIS TIME IT'S A
     VACUUM CLEANER.'

FX   HOOVER STARTING UP.

VLS   Being a charming likeable BBC personality now, I become emotional. The record has fond memories for me, this one reminds me of a domestic vacuum cleaner recorded in 1959 mono.

VLS   *(on radio to Parkinson)* OH, I'M SO NICE MICHAEL, SO NICE AND FRIENDLY AND EMOTIONAL AND FRIENDLY AND NICE AND... *(to mike)* I laugh so much at my BBC insincerity that I rupture myself, and quickly order a Hernia Kit over the phone, and buy it on credit with my Trusscard.

FX   PHONE BEEPS.

VLS   I pick up my eighth and final sound effect disc.

FX   PICKS UP PHONE. JEWISH VOICE, EVEN LESS CONVINCING THAN THE IRISH ONE: 'HELLO ALREADY, SUCH A BUSINESS, SO WHO NEEDS A WOMAN.'

VLS   It's my agent, Mori.

FX   JEWISH VOICE: 'VICTOR DARLING, WHY DO THIS TO ME ALREADY? I'VE TOLD ME TIME AND TIME AGAIN, I SAY "ME" I SAY "I CANNOT DO A JEWISH ACCENT". '
      VLS (INTO PHONE): 'I KNOW, I LIKE TO THINK I'M THE VOICE OF THEM ALL, IT'S PATHETIC REALLY. ANYWAY, ME PLAYING THE PART OF AN AGENT, WHAT'S COOKING?'
      JEWISH VOICE: 'WHAT'S COOKING? GREAT NEWS ALREADY. THERE'S BEEN A TERRIBLE NATIONAL DISASTER; WE GOT DEATH, WE GOT BURNING, WE GOT ROYALS CHOKING ON FISHBONES, WE GOT ORPHANED CHILDREN, BUT BEST OF ALL, WE GOT A CHARITY RECORD. IT'LL MAKE YOU LOOK CHARMING AND SINCERE AND CARING. LET ME EXPLAIN IN MY NORMAL VOICE.'

FX   *THE BODY IN QUESTION.*

VLS   Nothing brings a broader smile to the face of a sincere and caring media personality than a colossal natural disaster. Within hours, an appalling Charity Song will have been written, and more ITN cameras will be outside the recording studios than there are at the scene of the disaster itself. If you hear about such a recording, remember these tips:

1) Don't wait to be asked — just turn up.

2) Arrive looking ashen-faced and as though you've stayed up all night crying.

3) Attempt to block the camera's intrusion into your grief by covering the lens with your hand, but remember, keep those fingers well spread out so that the viewers can see who it is, and

4) In the studio, stand next to Tina Turner and on no account corpse or show any sign of insincerity as you sing your dollop of the banal lyric.

FX   EXTRACT OF SONG. VLS SINGS: 'I WAS TERRIBLY SORRY TO HEAR, IN ALL SINCERITY, THAT MRS THATCHER'S PET TORTOISE HAD SUDDENLY CEASED TO BE. IT'S A SHAME, IT'S A SHAME, THAT TORTOISE AIN'T TO BLAME.' CUT.

VLS   Fully indoctrinated with BBC smarm, I reach the apogee of broadcasting insincerity.

FX   RADIO ONE JINGLE.

VLS   *(impersonating Simon Bates):* 'GOOD MORNING, I'M BEAUTIFUL PEOPLE, YOU'RE BEAUTIFUL PEOPLE, I LOVE YA, LOVE YA, OKAY.'
      (close mike) Unfortunately I only do eight hours to the gallon on two star economy smarm, and ran out about...now.
      (à la Bates): 'I'VE A DEDICATION HERE FOR GRANNY LUMPEN FROM HER DAUGHTER PLEBS WHO LIVES IN THE SAME HOUSE AND SHE SAYS "WILL YOU SAY A SPECIAL HAPPY BIRTHDAY TO MY GRANNY WHO'S IN THE KITCHEN AT THE MOMENT?" WELL THE ANSWER IS... *(suddenly nasty)* NO. WHY DO YOU WANT TO SAY HELLO THROUGH A COMPLETE STRANGER WHEN SHE'S IN THE NEXT ROOM? YOU COULD DO IT YOURSELF PERSONALLY. JUST GET UP OFF YOUR FAT ARSE AND

GET INTO THE KITCHEN AND DO IT YOURSELF INSTEAD OF BOTHERING...'

FX   KLAXON SOUNDS. THEN THEME MUSIC FOR *IN THE PSYCHIATRIST'S CHAIR.* BBC CONTINUITY ANNOUNCER: *'IN THE PSYCHIATRIST'S CHAIR.* THIS WEEK ANTHONY CLARE TALKS TO ANOTHER RED-HOT FAVOURITE FOR THE LOONY BIN, VICTOR LEWIS SMITH.'

VLS AS ANTHONY CLARE: 'MY GUEST TODAY CRACKED UP THIS MORNING ON RADIO ONE. TELL ME VICTOR, WHY IS IT THAT YOU PERSIST IN THESE...DREADFUL...SHOCKING... TRULY AWFUL IMPERSONATIONS? TAKE ME FOR INSTANCE, I SOUND

NOTHING LIKE THIS, I NEVER HAVE DONE, AND BEGORRAS...'

FX   SINISTER STING.

VLS   He said 'Begorras'. I realise that he is one of the Murphia. Quick as a flash I rip off his face mask to reveal:

FX   SINISTER STING REPEATS.

VLS   Terry Wogan, swaying from side to side and saying 'Bejabers'. Yet another disguise. I rip off the face mask. This time it's Frank Delaney.

FX   *BOOKSHELF* THEME.

VLS AS FRANK DELANEY: 'WHAT HAVE SUSAN HILL, FRANK DELANEY AND HUNTER DAVIES GOT IN COMMON? ANSWER, THEY'VE ALL BEEN REMAINDERED, ALL ON...*BOOKSHELF.*'

MAKING PUNCH

A recipe by Paul Burbridge

PRESENTER	We come now to our cookery spot and today Quincey has come along to let us into the secret of making punch.
QUINCEY	Hi. Well, the basic ingredients are pretty simple and can be picked up around most high street shopping centres on a Friday evening. You'll need about one dozen men, separated roughly into two groups and then whisked up together in a large baking pub. Slop them all down with plenty of alcohol – it doesn't really matter what, anything that comes to hand, but the important thing to get right is the *quantity*. Mix this into a thick stupor and add a few large slices of ego. Turn up the temperature and just before serving pop in a tiny little misunderstanding to give it that final zing. That should produce an excellent punch for 40 people or even more.

My compliments to the chef.

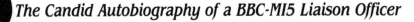

Hi, Thatcher

BLOODY MAT COWARD AGAIN

101

Dear Old Codgers
Why is there so much Mat Coward in this book? *(Mr Arnold Kunte Kinte, Crawley)*

Well, sir, we checked out with the contributors to *Loose Ends,* but half of them, like Craig Charles, Victoria Mather, Richard Jobson and Miss Coren, couldn't be bothered because there wasn't any money in it, whereas Mat Coward will do anything for eight quid cash in hand, no questions asked. Just no one tell the Inland Revenue, sir.

Back in the 1930s the radio show *Loose Ends* was believed by many in 'the Firm' to be the centre of a major communist cell. Today, Louse Nurds is best remembered for the scandalous 'on-air orgy' outrage which finally ended its fifty-year run, but in its heyday it was a viper's nest of sophisticates and satirists. Like the young ring-leader, Ted Sheridan, fresh down from Cambridge and, in those days, completely bald; and Margaret Howard, then as now Noel Edmonds' live-in lover, and an early suspect. Howard left the show before long, to serve Moscow (in another role perhaps?), and her place in the notorious studio B14 was taken by one Craig Charles, a black man and therefore, of course, genetically Marxist.

There were those in Room 101 — myself amongst them, I own — who came to the conclusion that Sheridan was transmitting secret messages to Eastern Europe through his opening monologues. Certainly, these seemed to serve no other obvious purpose. A thorough analsis by our lads in the decoding section failed to reveal anything at all; they reported that the scripts, as spoken by Sheddin, consisted of nothing but a random assortment of words, noises and punctuation. Could the wheezes and coughs hold any clue? I wondered. Sadly, we were never to find out. The officer assigned to their investigation passed on before

his work was complete. The post mortem found that he had been 'irritated to death'.

But many of us were far from satisfied. We turned our attention to another anomaly: why was it that every edition of Louche Ians featured a number of so-called 'guests'; guests whom no-one had ever heard of before, who had no apparent reason for appearing on the show, and who subsequently disappeared without trace? Could it be that Sharmaine and his henchmen were 'bumping off' intellectuals — or even smuggling them beyond the Iron Curtain?

Sadly we were never to know. There were many moles poking their heads above ground in those days, and we were soon moved on to another case: was *Going Places* a plot by pinko TV producers to boost their early evening audiences?

But the Lace Earns story has one, intriguing, post-script. Many years later, when I had been long retired, a woman named Thatcher became, incredibly, Her Majesty's Prime Minister — and, in time, Her Majesty herself. The name rang a bell, and, sure enough, on checking I found it to be the name used by one of the suspect Long Hour contributors. Was there a connection? Sadly, we were never to find out. Shortly before beginning this exciting book, I died and went to heaven.

CINEMA

Reviewed by **N. N. Sippy**

The Polish season at the National Film Theatre

I watched Broedjzsinky Sczxwyz's latest film, *Concrete in a Wardrobe*, which kicked off the Polish season at the NFT last Sunday.

Grainy black and white film and a wobbly sound track is all part of the stock-in-trade of the Polish film industry. The plot was simple enough and the archetypal stuff; Man lives in a bleak apartment. Buys dog. Locks it in suitcase. Lover discovers the half emaciated cadaver under the bed. She hangs herself. The apartment begins to decay. The man becomes obsessed with goldfish and tries to jam his head into the bowl. It's a poignant vignette which actually left my ears smarting and says something very profound about modern man's alienation from nature. Then Sczxwyz gives us an interesting twist.

At that exact point a woman sitting next to me who claimed to be the reviewer for the *Daily Telegraph* said, 'I don't know what the hell is going on here. Are the reels in the right order? I suppose the projectionist is pissed and is it any wonder...he's already seen it 63 times this week. I mean to say, there's always a streak of bearded piss

cavorting about on a beach next to a bleeding wardrobe and talking out of sinc., and then there's a cutaway shot of a baby eating razor blades, and then the screen divides into 50 identical split frame shots of a priest wanking over a potato, and then there's some anaemic actor in a black turtle neck sweater and dark glasses thrashing a lightbulb with a tennis racket, and then it cuts to a pregnant Slav who's caught her nipple in the escalator, and then there's a fish eye lens shot of the priest, who's now shacked up with a sailor who looks like Bernard Breslaw and who keeps spitting on his palms and looks guilty and keeps shouting 'Mother of Christ Forgive me', and then the film breaks and then an hour later they put it together again and then the bloke with a beard at the front who runs this so called cinema, and who is sitting in a conspicuous foetal position, laughs loudly in all the wrong places because he's pretending that he understands the subtleties of Polish humour in the Polish language and I just *wish* I could stop the film and turn a spotlight on him and say, 'Come on then, Mr Open University course in fucking Eastern Bloc culture, let's all share the joke then you bastard!,' and then the credits come up and everyone stays and reads them even though they're all in Polish when actually they want to piss off down to the pub and then there's a big caption that says 'FIN' and I'll be buggered if I've seen sight or sound of a fish for the past six hours.'

At that point she was removed from the theatre. Frankly, I enormously admired what the woman was saying. It reminded me of the scene in 1984, where the fat proletariat who rebels against the forces of an indoctrination

RADIO

Loose Ends

Nigel Fripp

RADIO 4 WITH NED SHERRIN

I listened with interest to Lo̶
tired old run of the mill gue̶
lacklustre performances by Jona̶
Bert Weedon's rendition of Una̶
false teeth fell out into the asht̶
delight. But why oh why should the̶
referred to all feminists as ugly and̶
with beards too ugly to get a man Eng̶
–erdink unusual vile sexual peccadil̶
actually in Ned Sherrin's mouth extra̶
cannot believe the goat consented to pr̶
RSPCA gave a full search for drugs whi̶
claimed kept it for the wool and shou̶
one of the Nolan Sisters claimed qu̶
said she most certainly had been bug̶
Steve Race. Who would have believed su̶
pleasant, affable man, My Music will ne̶
Wallace is half blind now as a result of S̶
horrific scenes in the green room befor̶
–turbation and gumming. Wallace b̶
Sherrin said he'd never met Steve Ra̶
hilarious photographs and Prince Ph̶
man in the mask at the Keiler par̶
'slitty eyes slitty slitty' forced his fi̶
she can't walk now since the colonic ir̶
–gasm ever quite like it. 'It's like a thou̶
faecal matter isn't a problem'. Gillian Rey̶
–terviewed the Bishop of Durham who conf̶
–cifix rammed very hard, very hard indee̶
way for a Bishop to behave. 'No', said the B̶
'your mouth you fat old Queen wi̶
dog and bone I want a taxi NOW do you̶
Phew! Radio 4 has never heard the like.

Have you ever wondered just how the BBC keeps track of listeners' tastes? Find out now, as we go ...

Behind the scenes with the audience researchers

The main tool of research is the man on the street face-to-face interview. We followed an interviewer on one of these vox pop missions.

RESEARCHER: Excuse me, sir, do you have a moment spare?

LISTENER: It'll take more than a moment, darling!

R: I wonder if I might ask you about your current listening habits?

L: Habits? Habits? Christ, you don't waste any time do you, sweetheart?

R: Would you say that you listen to BBC Radio a lot, or would you say you listen a little?

L: I'll say 'I do' for you, lovey!

R: Fine. Second question, which of the domestic services do you tune into most often?

L: Whoops, hello sailor! Ha ha ha ha! 'Ere — what are you implying?

R: Do you listen most often: in the bath, in the kitchen, in the car, or in the living room?

L: Not half gorgeous! All of the above, and you left out swinging from the chandelier! Whoops! Eh?

R: Do you stay tuned to one station all the time, or do you listen to various stations at various times?

L: God help us, I should say so! I'm an incurable knob-twiddler, you ask my wife! Or better still, I'll show you myself while she's out at evening classes — woho!

R: Moving on to specific programmes, did you hear last Saturday's edition of *Loose Ends*, presented by Ned Sheridan?

L: I should say I did. Bloody disgusting. It's nothing but endless innuendoes. All those so-called clever people from Cambridge, and that Ned Sheridan — a man who's been knighted by Her Majesty ought to have more concern for decent people, never mind all them Puppies, what about normal people? We're not all members of the Harpo club. You make me vomit you lot, you do! *(Listener terminates interview).*

MAT COWARD

Yes, we're fully satisfied with the British Broadcasting Corporation. We speak as one when we say 'It's the best bargain in Britain'.

We also listened in to the work of the duty officer

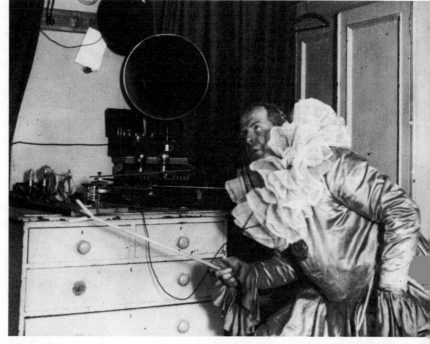

'Duty office ... yes ... yes ... I think it's called Loo Bends ... yes ... not that I listen to it myself. No, I don't let *my* kids listen either. No, no, I don't blame you. Disgusting. Mucus, that's right, I know. No they don't, you're so right, they don't care at all, nothing's sacred ... I know, quite right, well they even take the mickey out of us, you know ... that's right, duty officers, I dare say I'd take the mickey out of them if I had their expense account! ... No, I know, *I know* ... satire, that's it. Huh! No, I don't know either, vulgarity and being rude to the Queen, that's what it means as far as I can make out ... terrible ... she didn't? ... oh, no ... well, you tell your mother she has my sympathy ... Yes, I'll pass it on to the producer, not that anybody will take any notice — well, why should they? We're only the licence payers, I know, exactly what I say ... quite, love, quite ... I *know*, and he thinks he's so clever as well ... well of course he is, it's obvious when you know what you're looking for isn't it ... I was in the lift with him yesterday morning, worst luck ... yes he was, wearing it at that time in the morning, bold as you like ... rustling away it was ... My dear, it's the talk of the building, but nobody does anything ... they're all like him if you ask me ... all right dear, yes, I'll write it down and send it up ... quite, as you say, for all the good it'll do ... oh well, you're not alone anyway ... and my best to your poor mother ... they don't, they don't care, they don't ... goodbye then, ... yes, nice talking to you too...'

PHONE RINGS AGAIN

'Duty office ... who produces *what?* ... factsheet, what factsheet? ... Well I don't know do I? I'm not God am I? ..look in the *Radio Times* ... well if you're too mean to buy the *Radio Times,* you're not going to get your supplementary benefit factsheet are you? ... no ... *(hangs up)* ... Honestly, some people!'

Finally, **THE RATINGS SYSTEM,** the third method of divining audience appreciation, is worked out according to a complex but essentially simple formula: the producer decides what figure he'd like to have; he cuts it in half; he receives the numbers from the listening panel; he adds in his children's birthdays and his car registration number; finally, he rounds it up to 'around one million give or take' and points out that it's '20% more than the previous show in this slot had'.

MAT COWARD

Picture if you can, if you dare, such a scene. It is deep in the bowels of a monolithic and menacing building. The air is stale, the décor spartan, the only furniture a single, large wooden table surrounded by straight, stern chairs. The only source of comfort, a single, chipped jar of foetid water. It is early morning, but you would never know inside this bunker where no light ever enters. Many of the occupants of this room have seen no sleep, they are bleary-eyed and stubbled, and that is just the women. It is not a pretty scene.

At the head of the table sits a big, forbidding man with the air of a once-dashing officer gone slightly to seed. A stained cravat hangs askew at his neck. What once was hair is now but a wisp, his blue pullover as threadbare as his thatch, his chin, scarred by the blade, is spotted with tissue to stem the flow. Before this man speaks he has to cough to clear a throat ravaged by too many dry white wines. When finally he launches into a lengthy monologue, the others sitting round the table, all of them much younger than our one-time military man, just laugh. There is a sadness in this scene.

But the youngsters are impervious to such shabby melancholy. They do not even notice the slight, tragic flair of the trouser that sits hidden beneath the head of the table, the trouser shiny from one too many hasty pressings in a batchelor pad. This is in fact the bottom half of a suit bought, along with the rest of his wardrobe, in a glorious week when our man was still at the height of his career; that was the week that was. At the foot of this ensemble sits a pair of brown shoes, bought once in Bond Street, but scuffed now from years of drunken stumbles to the World's End. He doesn't stumble in this monologue though, he just keeps on and on. The youngsters just laugh.

But would they chuckle so, if they could see themselves? To the right of the grand old man sits a siren. A tall, some would say Amazonian figure, with a muddy brown mane tousled into an attempted Southfork sweep, she looks at times a little lost. Is she, as the windblown Meryl Streep strip, the riding boots and the flared skirt suggest, out of Africa? Or is she just fresh out of hairspray?

The voice, of course, is a give-away. A Luis Vuitton basketful of Victoria plums grown on the Yorkshire dales, but now ranging freely round rounded sloany tones. And she wears the clothes to match. Flouncy county might be one description of her style, or S.W. sexy. The colours though are a touch too bright, the bangles too big, the cheeks too ruddy for a true sophisticate. The labels, I'm afraid, are a touch too gauche. Anyone for Paris? A jolly girl at heart, this one.

Labels figure large in the life of another of the inmates of this cell. Simon Dee's lispy lovechild is just one of the labels that has been attatched to the young man who sits, always immaculately besuited, as if to mock the faded finery of the father figure. There are suits by the score, all of them scored with huge discounts from the ultra-hip designer shops of South Molton Street, for whom this young man is a talking advertisement.

And even at the ungodly hour at which this decidedly ungodly crew gather, the suits are very prominently, proudly and pedantically displayed. But is there actually anything inside them? That is yet to be conclusively proven. Still, despite the great mystery, the suits do their stuff. The loafers also loaf, the quiff quivers and the blazer blazes; all of which makes for great radio first thing in the morning.

Which is more than you could ever say about the man who is not there. His presence is felt in the room they call B14, but he is never seen. Instead this mysterious fellow despatches disgusting tapes from his northern hidey hole. Having once glimpsed this mythical beast of boredom, I know why he is so shy. He is the worst dressed man in the world.

LooseEnders

It seems that the only sartorial criteria applied by this mania is that nothing whatsoever is allowed to fit properly. Jeans, the type Tescos turn down, hang disconsolately off the large child-bearing hips to reveal that attractive expanse of flesh from the top of the buttocks, to the bottom of the too-tight, stained corduroy bomber jacket. Nice, drip-dry, Bri-nylon shirts, dyslexically buttoned, peek provocatively from odd angles. Dirty brown nylon socks, usually secreted beneath the acres of crumpled denim, sit and sweat uneasily inside plastic training shoes. Atop all this sits a pair of national healths, and a riot of greasy brown ringlets. All of the others in this room are simply glad that this monster is heard and not seen.

But it is hard not to notice the next female member of this tragic team. All things bright and bountiful might be one way to describe her style. Another might be to say that she dresses like the presenter of a TV programme for very young children, which in fact she used to be. So of course a whacky crop of hair, to prove how young she is, crowns every colourful and crazy outfit.

Primary colours clash mercilessly and noisily. Trousers too tight and too bright, are stuffed, then stuffed into plastic pointed pixie boots, that reek of Carnaby Street, and, despite improbable heels, do little to raise her diminutive stature. They just make it wobble a little. Which is understandable because there is lots on top, and on top of those come sweaters and scarves and big bomber jackets complete with belts and buckles and badges and bits all adding to the cacophony. Luckily for listeners, radio sets don't have screens, or else you would all be reaching for the volume control. The poor souls in that room in the mornings just have to avert their eyes.

Still, in that dark and dour dungeon, a little light relief is occasionally welcome. Maybe that is why all concerned tittered a little when the newcomer came. A dapper dilettante dandy, some might say. A jumped-up jock in silly clothes is an alternative version. With hair reminiscent of a plate of crinkle-cut chips, a jaw-line Jimmy Hill would joke about, and a voice like molten mugging, he cuts a dashing, if rather daft, figure.

donning a large, floppy, round red hat, a black jacket, a red skirt, and intolerably tarty three-tone shoes in blue, red and gold. This sober little ensemble was topped off by a gold lizard with bright red eyes, last seen crawling up her chest. It is not known whether the red eyes were designed to match her father's.

Usually, though, her clothes do not seem to be designed to match anything, especially each other. A rather peculiar mix of jumble sale, British Home Stores and Harrods, always finished off with her particular fetish, hooker heels. I can only suggest that her mother neglected her as a child.

The final regular languishing in that dreaded room is difficult to dissect sartorially because he is usually still in the process of dressing when he arrives, if he arrives. Essentially a typically scruffy scouser, he is known to own at least one pair of jeans which are either worn washed or unwashed, for variety. This young man does, though, possess a collection of caps. Most of them are of the terribly trendy baseball type, and worn predictably back to front. It is a good job that he has the hats, though, because at one point he suddenly sprouted a series of rather unsavoury stunted ponytails out of the back of his head. He claimed that these were

Sartorially he is a porridge of classic English eccentric with Japanese designer labels from the likes of Yohji Imatomato, Comedy Garçon and Ishe Meauntie. This would indeed be quite an impressive array, until you remember that he is in fact Scottish. It then becomes obvious that all of this expensive tat was undoubtedly begged, borrowed or, most likely, stolen from his various glamorous modelling assignments.

The next inmate of Room B24 has not, as yet, been asked to stroll the catwalk, though she recently walked towards the aisle in an outfit Ronald McDonald would have considered garish. This girl honoured her big brother's big day by

something to do with a job on television. Everybody, though, knew that could not be true. Whoever heard of a Liverpudlian with a job?

And whoever heard such a stylistically staccato bunch on the wireless before? This room without a view contains an almost matchless collection of odd characters, and a sartorial swathe to match. They have only one thing in common, they are together for only one reason. It is that cheque which once a week wings its way from the Corporation to these money-grabbing mercenaries. These are hoarded until the day that so much has been accumulated that they can go out on a stylistic orgy, and squander it all on a pair of socks.

KEEP YOUR ENDS LOOSE
R. Elms

OFFICE OF THE PRESIDENT
Mall Rd.,
Mayo Rd. Crossing
Rawal Pindi
Pakistan

BRITISH BRO
BROADCASTI
TEL
TELEGRAMS AND CA

AWAITING REPLY

Dear President Zia-ul-Haq of Pakistan,

May we take this opportunity to congratulate you on the very excellent way in which you rule your country with a rod of iron, and yet retain your legendary fairness and sense of humour. We, in Gt. Britain, rèfuse to believe the sort of sensationalist reportage to which your good self has been subjected in recent years. Mr. Malik at my local Indian restaurant has told me everything I care to hear thankyou very much Mr. President.

Mr. President. It would be an honour and a matter of some considerable joy to all of us here at BBC Broadcasting House if you so deemed it fit to write a FORWARD, in your own hand (with photograph), for the BBC 'Loose Ends' book we are writing. Ned Sherrin, the Presenter of the programme, has promised one, but he'salazy 'sod so we don't hold much hope there. Just a standard introduction will do. Something on the lines of : "I wish this book a great deal of success. I would tune in every week, but we cannot get the programme on World Service".

Please have one of your minions to send your superb photograph and manuscript (please, no more than 2 lines) to the above address marked to Sir Victor Lewis Smith and Lord Paul Sparks of (Dagenham near Fords) at ROOM NUMBER 7076. BBC BROADCASTING HOUSE.

Thankyou, oh, thankyou your very great Highness in anticipation of your firmness.

Yours truly,

VICTOR X paul

Sir Victor Lewis-Smith
Lord Paul Sparks (of Dagenham near Fords)

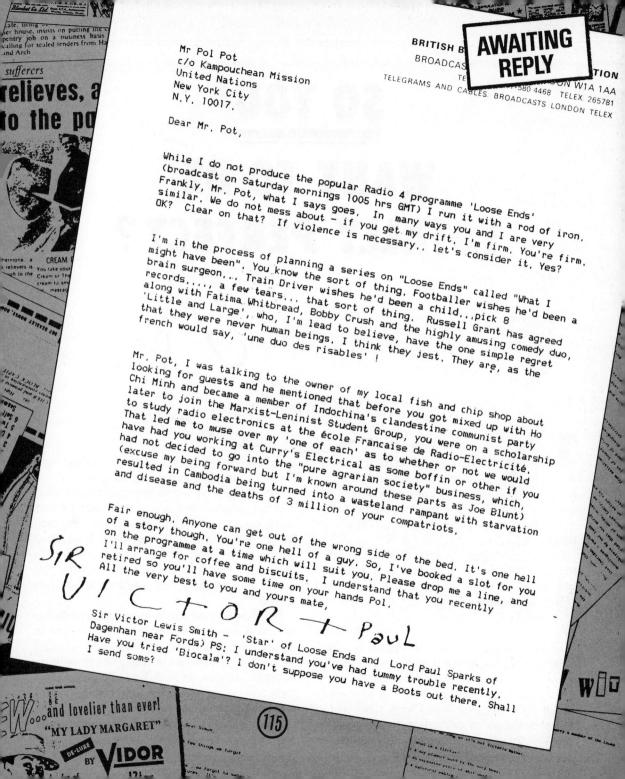

Mr Pol Pot
c/o Kampouchean Mission
United Nations
New York City
N.Y. 10017.

Dear Mr. Pot,

While I do not produce the popular Radio 4 programme 'Loose Ends' (broadcast on Saturday mornings 1005 hrs GMT) I run it with a rod of iron. Frankly, Mr. Pot, what I says goes. In many ways you and I are very similar. We do not mess about - if you get my drift, I'm firm, You're firm. OK? Clear on that? If violence is necessary.. let's consider it, Yes?

I'm in the process of planning a series on "Loose Ends" called "What I might have been". You know the sort of thing. Footballer wishes he'd been a brain surgeon... Train Driver wishes he'd been a child...pick 8 records...., a few tears... that sort of thing. Russell Grant has agreed along with Fatima Whitbread, Bobby Crush and the highly amusing comedy duo, 'Little and Large', who, I'm lead to believe, have the one simple regret that they were never human beings. I think they jest. They are, as the french would say, 'une duo des risables' !

Mr. Pot, I was talking to the owner of my local fish and chip shop about looking for guests and he mentioned that before you got mixed up with Ho Chi Minh and became a member of Indochina's clandestine communist party to study radio electronics at the école Francaise de Radio-Electricité, later to join the Marxist-Leninist Student Group, you were on a scholarship That led me to muse over my 'one of each' as to whether or not we would have had you working at Curry's Electrical as some boffin or other if you had not decided to go into the "pure agrarian society" business, which, (excuse my being forward but I'm known around these parts as Joe Blunt) resulted in Cambodia being turned into a wasteland rampant with starvation and disease and the deaths of 3 million of your compatriots,

Fair enough. Anyone can get out of the wrong side of the bed. It's one hell of a story though. You're one hell of a guy. So, I've booked a slot for you on the programme at a time which will suit you. Please drop me a line, and I'll arrange for coffee and biscuits. I understand that you recently retired so you'll have some time on your hands Pol,
All the very best to you and yours mate,

SIR
VICTOR + Paul

Sir Victor Lewis Smith - 'Star' of Loose Ends and Lord Paul Sparks of Dagenhan near Fords) PS: I understand you've had tummy trouble recently, Have you tried 'Biocalm'? I don't suppose you have a Boots out there. Shall I send some?

SO YOU
WANT TO BE
TOTALLY PERFECT?

Dear Old Codgers

My hubby has noticed that despite his letter there's still too much Mat Coward in this book. I have had sleepless nights. Can you help?

Well, ma'am, we contacted the editors and it seems he agreed to work for £4 a page, an offer they couldn't refuse. It's the way of the world, ma'am!

...That's understandable. In the old days, before I became totally perfect, that's what I wanted to be: totally perfect. Now that I am totally perfect of course the want has gone — and my only real desire in life is to pass on my knowledge to others whose need is great.

First of all, it's good to start off as near totally perfect as you can. I started off as near to totally perfect as it's possible to be, but needing — perhaps — just *un soupbowl de* touching up around the perimeters.

So the first thing I did was become a Bishop. Think seriously about this one before you take it on: it means a big commitment, and not everyone is willing or able to pay the price. In my case, the price was eight dollars paid to the American Fellowship Church for my Legally Valid Clergy Card, and a long peak-rate phone call to Rev. Ted Swenson in California for spiritual counselling. If you're going to follow this path, make sure you pick the right church: Some, apparently, demand celibacy — which means you have to profane from necking with hot chicks — and in others you have to wear weird, uncool threads. In some churches, you even have to believe in God, although Rev. Ted assured me that in his outfit 'we have a lot of people with an agnostic bent who have joined us and later felt that they have achieved considerable spiritual growth'.

I tried out a lot of glamorous occupations during my quest for perfection: becoming a pop star (Alvin Stardust even went so far as to describe me as 'rather brown, really', which is something of a recognition of genius in the music world); a footballer; a game show host; a comedian and a society photographer. I even auditioned for the part of James Bond, though eventually I had to turn that one down for contractual reasons (I wasn't offered one), and the studio went for the number two, Timothy Dalton. I realise that a lot of movie-goers were upset about that, but I hope they will respect my need for personal privacy.

During my search for absolute and total wonderfulness, I escorted some of the planet's most beautiful women, like Samantha Fox (Sammy-babes and I had a little joke together: every time we met I used to say 'My name's Mat Coward' and she would quip 'Who the hell are you?'! What a dame!). I quickly learnt that when it comes to self-improvement, it's not who you are that counts, it's what you look like. The whole thing is a matter of image. And, hey — having a striking image doesn't mean going around looking like a Yorkshire miner!! (Told you I was a comedian. Stan Boardroom thought I was, and I quote, 'A very funny sort of person indeed', and you can't get a recommendation higher than that.)

So if you're to follow in my footsteps to the top, become totally perfect and start dating girls with inch-long nipples, you're going to need the right image. To give you a guide, I've included here a kind of Totally Perfect Fact sheet all about me. Obviously, you shouldn't copy it exactly — if you start calling yourself Mat Coward, for instance, you will only cause disappointment and heartbreak to the people you meet — but it should give you a few useful wrinkles.

NAME: Bishop Mat Coward.

AGE: As old as my knees. Between 15 and 40.

NATIONALITY: Citizen of the world, daddy-o.

HEIGHT: Exactly spot-on for purposes of sexiness and grace.

WEIGHT: ... I'm waiting ...

DISTINGUISHING FEATURES: Aura of total perfection, extreme sexiness, and hipness to a degree never before encountered.

AMBITION: Perfect people don't have ambitions – it's one of the sacrifices I've just had to come to terms with.

MODE OF DRESS: From the top: hair, roughly plastered to head, but sticking out here and there; tortoiseshell specs, containing smoked glass, held together with sticky-tape — *très in le mood!*; heavily insulated anorak or windcheater, turd brown, waterproof (as far as I know — I've never washed it); T shirt with slogan — 'My folks went to the Outer Hebrides and all I got was abandoned there in an iron safe'; vest; bottle-green hairy trousers (NB not flares — they went out in 1985); Y Fronts with 'bag o'nuts' motif (spare pair coincidentally identical in design — that should squash a few rumours I hope); 100% nylon socks with pictures of bare ladies on them; bakeolite hiking-style surgical boots, with hidden compasses and 'Gucci-Korea' designer label on sole.

CATCHPHRASES: 'Excuse me mate, are you Carol Barnes?'; 'Of course you're busy, pal, we're all busy, this will only take ten minutes'; 'No, I don't drive' (in answer to question 'Do you have a CV?').

FAVE FOOD AND DRINK: Monster munches and light ale, respectively.

FAVE POP SOUNDS: Whatever was No. 1 five years ago this week — I like to keep up.

FAVE COLOUR: Brown.

FAVE TV SHOW: *Price Is Right* (when I watch TV it is for instruction, not entertainment).

FAVE RADIO: Simon Bates' *In The Small Wee Hours* (Radio 2, New Year's Eve).

FAVE MEMBER OF THE ROYAL FAMILY: Ted Sheridan, presenter of Loo Sends

So there you have it. Following the path to perfection won't be easy — nobody promised you a rose garden — and it is full of pratfalls where the unwary or uncool could come unstuck. It will mean hard work, sacrifice and dedication. But in the end it will be worth it: stick with it and you could end up with a lifestyle like mine. Or, as many kind and helpful celebrities have put it to me over the last couple of years, 'Get out of here you little wanker, and go and bother someone else.'

Due to imminent deadline there will be no heading for Part VII. NO joke...they're taking this out of my hands as I speak. Give me a pen.

Look! only need a minute – Don't take that paper away

Our Belling Cosi-glo with the simulated real-look coal fire (two-bar model).

I won't beat about the bush, as a council tenant who bought, I didn't vote Mrs Thatcher in for nothing. One thing we don't require in Warley, thank you very much, are f'ing and blinding squatters. Fortunately I had the presence of mind to take home from Mr Sippi's a small but effective tactical nuclear weapon which he had secreted in the laundry basket for just such a purpose. 'Right,' I said to Brenda ... 'How dare they, HOW DARE THEY smash their way in through my aluminium framed patio doors as advertised on television by the very excellent Ted Moult. How dare they? I'm going to sort them out with a bit of good honest coppering and send them off with a flea in their ears.' Not that I had fleas, you understand, it's what the *Reader's Digest* often refers to as a metaphorical flea. I always say, it pays to increase your word power.

Quick as a flash, I was up those stairs and confronting a couple having, as it were if you don't mind thank you, a barbecue in the bath. 'WHAT DO YOU THINK THIS IS ... PLEASE,' I said in my firm and authoritative voice, 'I'LL TELL YOU WHAT IT IS ... IF YOU DON'T MIND I'LL TELL YOU ... IT'S A FIASCO,' I said. 'YOU CAN'T RUN A BARBECUE LIKE THAT,' I said. 'WHAT YOU NEED IS THOSE LITTLE CLINKERS OF CHARCOAL. YOU CAN GET THEM FROM ALL LEADING

HARDWARE STORES. IF ANYONE'S HAVING A BARBECUE IN MY HOUSE IT'LL BE DONE PROPERLY OR NOT AT ALL. YOU'RE NOT SHOWING ME UP IN FRONT OF THE NEIGHBOURS.'

Then I said to Brenda, I said, Brenda, have you noticed something, I said, have you noticed that all our new occupants are ladies with their hair cut short and wearing scruffy men's Army Surplus baggy clothes?' I said, I said I know what we've got here, I said. Anyway, cut a long story short, I said what you lot need is a man, that's what you need, or maybe even one each, I said. You don't want to fill your heads up with all that equality nonsense and G spots, and then I broke into that song made popular by

of an excellent consumer electrical product called the Ladyshave? It only takes a minute over the kitchen sink, and you can wash away unsightly tufts down the plughole with the tea-leaves, I said. Brenda does it every three hours and I don't see why, MADAM, you shouldn't follow in my good lady wife's footsteps. What you need is a no-nonsense hubby to teach you what's what, I said, and I was just about to follow that up with my the trouble is you're too ugly to marry routine when suddenly one of them shouted 'Women against male violence', jumped on me, and practised sundry martial arts on my person, leaving me paralysed all points south of the navel. I THINK it was at that moment that I

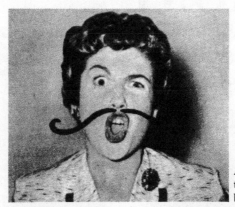

A lady who has never sampled the luxury of the twin rotary-bladed fine-mesh Philishave.

Maurice Chevalier called 'Girls Were Made to Love and Kiss', and followed it up swiftly with 'Thank Heavens for Little Girls' for which I adopted a Parisian accent, in an attempt to appease their womanly anger because they'd told me they were angry about men getting all the jobs. JOB I said, you wouldn't know the meaning of the word my girl, I said. Being a wife and mother, that's the only job you want to worry yourself about. And I'll tell you a few home truths, I said, I said have you never heard of facial hair removal? Have you never heard

lost my self-control, and allowed them to place a necklace on me. Not your usual run of the mill necklace this. More your crossply radial with a considerable amount of fire pouring out of it. 'Call this a fair trial?' I said. 'Why, you wouldn't last a minute in the Law Society'. Then everything went black.

Will Harold Coaltart escape from the clutches of the Warley Feminist Collective? Turn to p.127 to find out.

THE INGRAMS DEAF AID CO. RADIO AWARD CEREMONY

LOOSE ENDS SWEEPS THE BOARD

Award winners include:

Ned Sherrin – winner of the Golden Speculum for Most Creative Use of a Surgical Appliance on the Wireless.

Carol Thatcher – winner of the Silver Bougie for Most Convincing Outside Broadcast Compiled in a BBC Studio Using Sound Effects Records.

Mr Gardhouse – winner of the Bronze Pudenda for Most Stylish Visual Effects on a Radio Programme.

Jonathan Ross – winner of the Golden Handshake for allowing his name to be linked with *Loose Ends*, even though he's never appeared on it since he got to be a famous TV star (this award presented by the *Loose Ends* staff).

And, last and least,

Victor Lewis Smith – Personality Most Desperate to Get Out of Radio.

'In my 30 years on the beat I have never seen anything so disgusting in all my life.'

Relive now those emotional moments as he accepts his award, the Germoloid Golden Suppository, presented to him at the Deptford Special Clinic by TV Personality Steve Race and a woman with white teeth, a bronzed face and large breasts.

———————●———————

Thank you, thank you. Your Royal Highness, Chief Barker, Mr President, Pussy Cat Willum, Members of the Press, Myra Hindley, Layjennulmun. Yes I did say layjennulmun, layjennulmun. I said it because high-class artistes, the calibre of Marti Caine, Bobby Crush and Jimmy Tarbuck all say layjennlmun, layjennulmun, and they are all Water Rats layjennulmun, which means, layjennulmun, that they give a lot of money to Charity without letting anybody know about it...So how is it that we all know then layjennulmun? Layjennulmun, it's a paradox.

Frankly, your Royal Ma'am....smarm. With a twinkle in your eye, the way you stayed in your Council House when the bombs was dropping, God bless you Ma'am, just nobody mention anything about the shoplifting, God bless you Ma'am.

Layjennulmun, humbled...darlings...only a small cog in the wheel...travelled each and every byway layjennulmun...major open heart surgery layjennulmun...would it spoil some vast eternal plan layjennulmun...without whom, backroom boys...you sweet wonderful people layjennulmun ...cannot be here tonight... humbled layjennulmun, HUMBLED...*(PAUSES TO SQUIRT AMMONIA INTO EYES WITH EYE DROPPER, BECOMES EMOTIONAL)*..sixty years in the business layjennulmun...one day at a time sweet Jesus...man and boy layjennulmun...like to thank...Ronnie Renald...Clodagh Rodgers...Monty Modlyn... Keith Harris and Orville...Archbishop Makarios...Dorothy Squires...Chris Kelly layjennulmun...où sont les neiges d'antan layjennulmun...Wally Stott...all day long I'd iddle iddle um layjennulmun...Nina and Frederick layjennulmun...point d'exclamation et point virgule layjennulmun!;...given his life...don't deserve layjennulmun...humbled... HUMBLED.

Finally layjennulmun...given my life to radio ...photograph well when back lit layjennulmun ...move well on camera... available for work layjennulmun...adverts, voice-overs, any TV producers in the audience layjennulmun?... Shake 'n' Vac...Milk Chocolate Buttons... contemplating nose job layjennulmun... desperate layjennulmun, desperate...these hands layjennulmun...once the real hands playing the piano on Thunderbirds layjennulmun...inside Zippy on Rainbow layjennulmun...desperate layjennulmun desperate....

121

DR TREFUSIS'S SEMINAR ON THE OCCASION OF THE OSCAR CEREMONY

A transcription by Stephen Fry

I HAVE BEEN encouraged by my producer to say a few words on the subject of the Oscar ceremony. It is an invariable rule on the wireless that all those speaking of the Oscars ceremony open their remarks with the words: 'Behind all the hype and the superlatives the Oscar ceremony means big money', as if they have somehow surprised a secret out of the event by sheer dogged journalistic cunning. What they mean is that behind the blatant and vulgar attempt to make money lie hype and superlatives. If it didn't make money, the Americans wouldn't countenance it for a moment.

The Oscars in fact mean a tremendously small amount to me, so I shall use the occasion merely as a springboard for some severely offensive and bigoted remarks that I have been treasuring up in a small drawer in the bottom of my black heart for some many years now, and confine my remarks on the subject to

the thought that if Americans are mankind's supreme achievement, as they appear sincerely to believe themselves to be, and goodness knows they have the money, mouth and weaponry to back such a view up, then it is surely no exaggeration to propound the theory that mankind is on course for eternal damnation. That is as it may be, I have no particular esteem or fondness for the race of man, and I must suppose it deserves no other fate; however, it would not be seemly of me if I failed to shed a passing tear at what might have been, and sigh a mournful sigh at the frustration and disappointment of all the hopes this once proud species cherished for their advancement and improvement.

It was Clemenceau, was it not, the Tiger, who made the remark that America had moved from barbarism to decadence without the intervening stage of civilisation, and I would scarcely dare to improve upon a felicity from the lips of so distinguished a statesman and wit, but I would certainly take pleasure in sharing this thought with you: how strange that a nation, such as America, compounded as it is by uniformly charming and engaging citizens (such, at least, has been my experience of them) all, as individuals, really most entertaining and entrancing, should, as it were *en masse,* present an identity, a purpose and a character to the world so grotesque, so unseemly, so repellent that were Attila the Hun presented with their world vision he should have blenched and backed away. How is it that the elements so mixed in what history has been pleased to call this melting-pot, all so harmless, freedom-loving and enchanting of themselves, can—in the ferment of the crucible itself—precipitate all that is tyrannical and disgusting to persons of sensibility? It is as if we were to place violets, roses and lavender in a pot overnight and return to them the next morning to find that they had turned themselves into one gigantic cowpat.

To love Americans and yet despise with a contempt that frightens even myself the nation as a corporate

entity, how can I square this with myself? Perhaps America has done some good in the world, I try to convince myself. They gave enormous service and sacrifice to us during the Second World War. But the Russians gave of even more service and sacrifice and at least they don't belabour us with sanctimonious nonsense and inedible fried chicken, they at least are capable of attaining their base self-serving and greedy ends without recourse to hypocrisy, greasy cant and farcical language. Few countries have a worse history of religious and political oppression than this land of the free, the country where you are branded a communist if you can read the *New York Times* to yourself without moving your lips. Perhaps it is not their fault. They are brought up in the tragic and erroneous belief that the Declaration of Independence is a pattern of English prose: they are bidden swear allegiance to as revoltingly banale a piece of candy-striped drapery as one could find outside one of the emporia that Messrs Woolworth and company have inflicted upon an unwilling Europe: above all

they have unleashed upon themselves the nonsensically ill-thought-out proposition that they have an inalienable right to the pursuit of happiness, a concept whose internal paradoxes they have chosen not to explore, with the result that they have found that they have indeed pursued happiness: they have pursued that rare and beautiful creature right out of their home continent, pursued and harried it almost out of existence in their insane and egotistical rush for self-fulfilment, self-aggrandisement, self-improvement, self-importance and self-serving selfishness.

There, I've had my say. Charming people, taken on their own—but as a nation a compound of all that is worst in humanity. But I shall leave on an encouraging note: you are not the worst, America: one nation has a worse record of cant, humbug, nationalism and stupidity written on the pages of its long and inglorious history and that nation is, of course, Great Britain. If you have been, good morning.

ARE YOU
A *LOOSE ENDS* KINDA GUY?

Everyone who is anyone wants to get in on the Loose Neds phenomenon! Even Her Gracious Majesty the Queen has been heard to remark that she would give her 'eye teeth and my last pair of knickers' for just five minutes of being grilled by 'that nice Mr Ned'. But could *you* fit in with the crazy funsters of studio B14? Find out with our easy-to-do personality quiz ...

1. Do you have ...?
a) a speech impediment
b) a famous parent: (and/or big tits)
c) the tiniest hint of personality or talent
(NB: Only one of the above qualifications is necessary; candidates with all three will be disqualified).

2. Who do you consider the world's most utterly sophisticated human being?
a) Ned Sherrin
b) Robert Elms
c) Mat Coward

3. One of these people has *real* class. Which one?
a) Stephen Fry
b) Carol Thatcher
c) Victor Lewis Smith

4. You are organising a soirée for *Loose Ends* regulars. What do you serve to drink?
a) just champagne
b) champagne, vodka and Perrier
c) a choice of brown and mild, or Bacardi and Lucozade — the first drink included in the ticket price

5. You are invited to a *Loose Ends* bring a bottle party. What do you bring?
a) a specimen — because it's terribly wacky and probably hasn't been done before
b) some Perrier, because you saw it advertised in *The Face* and you're hoping to impress Robert Elms
c) a pint of Bacardi and Lucozade, just in case no-one else brings any

6. Which of the following catch-phrases do you use most often?
a) Yo, home boy
b) Shake yo' boody, daddio
c) Yo dirty wotten swine yo, yo have deaded me my capingtain

7. Your daughter or sister announces that she plans to marry a member of the *Loose Ends* team. Do you ...?
a) Say OK, as long as it's not Victor Lewis-Smith
b) Say OK, as long as it's not Craig Charles
c) Say OK, as long as it's not Victoria Mather

8. What is a Filofax?
a) a day planner used by the very busy
b) an expensive piece of shit used by wank pots
c) a satirical emblem used by writers with small imaginations and tight deadlines

9. How would you class yourself, acronym-wise?
a) a YUPPIE
b) a DINKY
c) a (hush) PUPPIES (Pissed-Up Poseur Participating In Endless Swank)

10. Do you own ... ?
a) a designer wardrobe
b) an ordinary wardrobe, full of designer clothes
c) designer piles

11. What do you call the room where you have a ▮▮▮▮▮ ?
a) the loo
b) the jacks
c) the kitchen

12. In your opinion, what quality should the ideal *Loose Ends* guest possess?
a) charm
b) wit
c) a window in her diary for next Saturday morning

HOW DID YOU SCORE?

I didn't. I stayed in and listened to *Loose Ends*.

Mostly A's: Not really very groovy are you? Unless you can produce a famous parent or a pretty special pair of tits from somewhere, I'd say forget it.

Between 14 and 901: Wowza! You're too hip even for us! Try *Breakaway,* with Bernard Falk.

In the range of 25% to 29%: Not bad, but you need to boost your swing quotient. (Or should that be swing your boost quotient?).

Mostly D's: You've done the quiz wrong. Please send photo and CV urgently.

ROSINA, LADY MADDING,
at home at Eastwold House

*reminisces to Dr Trefusis's amanuensis
Stephen Fry*

I live here alone in what, when I was a girl, used to be called the Dower House. I suppose I am technically a dowager, though my son Rufus, the fourth earl, is not yet married. I love the country, it's very peaceful here. I am surrounded by photographs of my past. On the piano I have a photograph of myself dancing with David, the Prince of Wales — later of course Edward the Eighth and subsequent Duke of Windsor. David was a very bad dancer, always trod on one's toes and I remember he once crushed the metatarsal bones in the foot of a girl-friend of mine — discreet lesbianism was fashionable at the time.

Here's a photograph of Noël Coward — darling Noël as we always called him. He was a very witty man, you know — it's a side of him not many people are aware of. I recall an occasion when I came on to the dance-floor of Mario's in Greek Street wearing a very daring frock, a frock that revealed more of my décolletage than was then considered proper—now of course I dare say it would raise nothing more than an eyebrow—but at the time it was very wicked. I came on to the floor and darling Noël came up to me and said 'Rosina'—he always used to call me Rosina—it is my name, you must understand. 'Rosina,' he said in that voice of his, 'Rosina, where did you find such an alluringly low-cut torso?' This was Noël's little way.

The portrait above the fireplace was made when I was in Paris—Claude my husband was Ambassador in the late 1920s. I used to hold very literary parties at the embassy: Plum and Duff Cooper, Scott and Garret Fitzgerald, darling Geoffrey Chaucer of course, Adolf Hitler and Unity Mitford, Gertrude Stein and Alice B. Topless, Radclyffe Hall and Angela Brazil—they could always be relied upon to attend. And of course O. Henry, James Joyce and Cary Grant. I remember F. E. Smith, later Lord Birkenhead of

course, that's his picture there, just below the dartboard, F. E. used to say, 'All the world and his live-in lover go to Rosina's parties', which pleased me very much. Later, when Claude and I went to India to take up the Vice-Regency, I met Gandhi, with whom I used to play French cricket—he was awfully good at cricket, as a matter of fact: Claude always used to say 'what the loin-cloth industry gained, the wicket-keeping industry lost.' Pandit Nehru was very impressive too, though if Edwina Mountbatten is to be believed his length was too variable for him ever to enter the ranks of Indian leg-spin immortals.

The large bronze statue of the nude male which stands on top of the synthesiser is of Herbert Morrison the Cabinet Minister. I use it to hang my bracelets on when I'm playing at the keyboard now. I spend a lot of time here in this room, remembering the past. Silly Poles Hartley, L. P. Hartley, you know, once said that the past is a foreign country, but I don't agree. The food was better for a start, and the people didn't smell. People often tell me I was one of a spoilt generation, rich, beautiful, idle, parasitical. It is true that I had every conceivable luxury lavished upon me during my life, met many famous and influential people, saw many exciting places and never did anything more taxing than organise large house-parties. But you know, despite that, if I had my time over again I wouldn't change a thing. Regrets? A few. I shouldn't have let dear T. E. Lawrence borrow my motor-bicycle. I'm tired now. Let me rest.